Mike Rowe

Biography

How I came to hear it

Santana Simmons

TABLE OF CONTENTS

Chapter 1: INTRODUCTION

I arrived at BWI's long-term parking lot 25 minutes before my aircraft was scheduled to depart. This would have happened back in 1988. June, I believe. I had baggage to check and security to go through, but if I hustled, I could still make it. There was just one problem: I couldn't get out of my automobile. That was the oddest thing. The door wasn't locked or jammed. The door was open, but I was imprisoned in my seat until the man on the radio said his magic words. Words that would enable me to grab my belongings from the trunk and race to the gate. Finally, these words were spoken.

"And now, you know the rest of the story."

How many times did I sit in parking lots and driveways long after I got at my destination, waiting for Paul Harvey to say those words? Too numerous to count. I missed my flight that day because of his immensely compelling radio show, The Rest of the Story, and ever since then, I've wanted to write stories that can't be turned off or put down until the finish. Stories that cause people to be late.

I will have more to say about Paul Harvey later. For the time being, I'd want to thank him for inspiring The Way I Heard It, the podcast whose name is also the title of the book you've just started. The mysteries in this book, like The Rest of the Story, recount actual stories about renowned people you may or may not be familiar with. Your task is to figure out who or what I am talking about before I finish. Inside, you'll find thirty-five puzzles taken from my show.

Many of these secrets were written in the heart of America—in its greasy spoons, motel rooms, and train stations. Others were written high above the fruited plain as I flew about hosting one event after another. But here's the funny thing. While penning mysteries amid the friendly sky, something mysterious happened to me. Time became compressed. Distances began to shrink. How many times have I started writing on the tarmac at SFO, only to look up a few minutes later, surprised to be landing at JFK? Too numerous to count.

Imagine myself at 37,000 feet…

My laptop is open, a light is on above me, and everyone else is sleeping. I chose a corner diner instead since the food is better, but you get the point—half of this book was written while on the road. The other half—the grout—was mixed right here on my kitchen table.

Perhaps you can picture it as well?

A fire cracks and crackles in the background, fog sweeps in from beneath the Golden Gate, and my trusty dog, Freddy, gnaws on my slippers as I battle with the topic that has been bothering me: why did I write about the people I did? The more I thought about what that something was, the more I realized certain unexpected connections—personal connections I hadn't recognized from 37,000 feet or at Mel's lunch counter. Invariably, these links began to rhyme, and the mosaic began to shift. The grout and tiles become equally crucial.

You've already met Freddy, and you'll see him again in the pages to come. He is a good guy. You will meet my parents, girlfriend, and my high school mentor. Along the way, you'll hear stories about Dirty Jobs and a slew of lesser-known shows that still haunt me on YouTube. I've tried to forget, but can't. In all situations, each story is told as I heard it. If you've heard it differently, I'm fine with it, and I hope you are, too.

By the way, I'm also attempting to visualize you. Is this creepy? I hope not.

I envision you checking into a lovely bed-and-breakfast—perhaps in Oregon, Texas, or perhaps England or France. You've arrived late and exhausted from your journey. You've started a fire and settled into bed. This dog-eared and soiled book is currently on your bedside table. You pick it up. You begin to read. When you glance up, the fog has cleared, the fire has been extinguished, and the sun has appeared exactly where the moon had been minutes before. You're wondering where the night went.

On Monday morning, at the water cooler, you might tell one of these anecdotes to a friend. They'll probably raise an eyebrow and exclaim, "Wow!" Is that actually how it happened? If I were you, I'd respond, "You better believe it. "That's how I heard it."

Chapter 2:THIS ISN'T FUNNY

Corporal Kaminsky was hung dangerously on an improvised utility pole, forty feet above the icy ground. In the dim light of a crescent moon, he squinted to finish his duty and fought gravity.

As a member of the 1104th Engineer Combat Group, Kaminsky was accustomed to such duties. He was not used to doing it thus close to the enemy. You see, the very pole to which this corporal clutched was installed in Belgium. Specifically, in the Ardennes forest. Just beyond the trees, a sizable portion of the German Army was prepared to launch a massive offensive known as the Battle of the Bulge.

They were so close that Kaminsky could smell them: an odorous stew of fuel, bratwurst, and boiling cabbage flooded his nose. He could hear them too. They'd been playing propaganda tapes all night: an ugly mix of the German national hymn, the crazed Führer's latest rantings, and the beautiful voice of Axis Sally, encouraging our lads to lay down their guns and submit.

As he pulled the final wire around the last screw that would transport the current to a slightly different broadcast, he heard a sharp mutter from the sentry below him. "This isn't funny, Kaminsky!" This made the young corporal smile.

Kaminsky shimmied down the pole, took one final look up at the massive loudspeaker he'd just placed, and laughed. The sentry shook his head as Kaminsky returned to battalion headquarters.

Kaminsky sifted through a little package of vinyl 78s, looking for the ideal choice for such an occasion. His gaze fell on a classic, and he chuckled again.

A switch was switched, a dial was turned, and the wall of sound emanating from Kaminsky's loudspeaker boomed throughout the icy woodland. Adolf Hitler's racial rants were quickly drowned out by the iconic refrain: "Toot, Toot, Tootsie, goodbye!"

Toot, Tootsie, don't weep!

Kaminsky observed the war-torn boys peeking out of their foxholes like curious prairie dogs. The absurdity of the scenario took a few moments to sink in, but eventually the irony flooded over the troops, and laughter broke out. One serenaded Nazis in the middle of a conflict, motivated by their crazy hatred of Jews. That was funny!

Following the war, he found work as a writer and comedian. He established himself in Hollywood for the next two decades. Finally, he had the opportunity to do what he was born to do: direct.

His initial attempt nearly gave the studio a heart attack. He wrote the screenplay himself, but the suits weren't amused. "That is not funny," they stated. But of course, Kaminsky understood what that meant: he had a winner! He stuck to his guns. He dug in his heels. Before long, Americans were thumping their toes to upbeat songs like "Springtime for Hitler" with punchy lyrics like "Don't be stupid, be a smarty, come and join the Nazi Party!"

Perhaps that was bad taste. Maybe it was too early. Those who were put off by Kaminsky's directorial debut had plenty of opportunities to be offended—on the big screen, the little screen, and, of course, the Great White Way.

I've never played "Toot, Toot, Tootsie" in a forest full of Nazis. But, with the help of three high school friends, I did sing it in four-part harmony before a variety of captive audiences in Baltimore, Maryland. Nursing homes were our favorite location, followed in no particular order by hospitals, bathrooms, VFW halls, prisons, elevators, stairwells, and crowded restaurants.

At Baltimore's Overlea High School, our larger-than-life music instructor, Mr. King, had introduced us to the mystical joys of barbershop harmony. Mr. King was a great baritone in a quartet named the Oriole Four, and he was known in the trade as the "King of the Barbershoppers." We acquired an excellent repertoire of chestnuts under his tuition, including "Margie," "Lida Rose," "The Sunshine of Your Smile," and "Sweet Adeline"—unapologetically emotional songs that would have made other teenagers cringe. But we adored those songs and quickly created our own band.

We referred to ourselves as "Semi-Fourmal" since we donned tuxedos and tennis shoes. We purposefully misspelled "formal" because there were four of us and we were quite clever. Chuck sang lead. I sang bass. Bobby and Mike sang baritone and tenor, respectively.

Every Tuesday night, a hundred men from many walks of life congregated in the old gymnasium at Johns Hopkins Hospital. Doctors, carpenters, lawyers, plumbers, accountants, dentists, teachers, Democrats, Republicans, Protestants, Catholics, and Jews—a diverse group of men whose deep love of four-part harmony was matched only by their love of God, country, and beer. I will never forget the first time I heard them sing. The Nazis may have been taken aback by the sound of "Toot, Toot, Tootsie" bursting through the forest on that chilly winter night, but the sound of a hundred soldiers singing the same song in perfect harmony would have astounded them. It was unlike anything I had ever heard. A sound filled the air with buzzing and crackling overtones. The sound was so rich, full, and clearly masculine that it made the hairs on your arms rise up.

Ultimately, the sound drew me into show business.

After rehearsal, we'd follow the men to Johnny Jones, a Highlandtown tavern, for another type of singing. Improvised harmonizing isn't always appealing. However, it is enjoyable to do and an excellent method to learn old tunes. Johnny's featured a room full of square tables—just enough space for four men to harmonize at point-blank range. There were songs about mothers, flying machines, and friends who would never abandon you.

Kids today believe they know everything. Back in 1979, we were no different. But after a few visits to Johnny's, I began to reconsider the cost of freedom.That was something I learnt from an elderly tenor named Gus, who had once been among the missing. Brave guys like Gus had learnt the hard way what I learned simply by standing by them and singing: you're only as good as the man next to you.

But, as Mel Brooks would tell you, courage is a funny thing. You never know where you might discover it. Or whether you'll have it when you need it most.

Chapter 3: A HERO UNDER THE INFLUENCE

Charlie, like everyone else at Ground Zero, was in the wrong place and at the wrong time. He'd spent the entire day in the kitchen, supervising a team of thirteen junior bakers who were cranking out breads, cakes, pies, and pastries for a crowd that never seemed to leave. Charlie had always wanted to create a name for himself in a prestigious kitchen. He'd traveled to a distant, well-known city with high hopes of success. Those dreams were finally coming reality. Charlie was the chief baker at one of the world's most prestigious restaurants, where he enjoyed his work and was dedicated to impressing his clients.

To clarify, Charlie was inebriated on the day in issue. His blood alcohol level a few hours after impact would have revealed an almost unbelievable rate of consumption. But that's the point: Charlie's drinking happened after the hit, not before. Who can truly blame him? When the walls and floor shook around him, Charlie realized something had slammed into the high structure—something large. And when he witnessed the depth of the destruction, he remained calm. He simply retired to the bar of his now-empty restaurant to have what he knew would be his final drink.

For Charlie, the possibilities were limitless. There were Beaujolais and sherry, Drambuie and absinthe, cognac and Armagnac, countless aisles of schnapps, and international beers. The majority of it, however, consisted of ancient Irish whiskey. Ah, yes. That was exactly what the doctor ordered. The ideal elixir to prepare Charlie for the task at hand—one he believed he was obligated to complete.

Charlie crushed half the bottle and transferred the remainder to a big flask. Then he filled a sack with bread and pastries and slowly climbed to the top floor.

"Follow me," he instructed. "I know the way out."

There was chaos up top. Charlie did everything he could to reassure his clients. First he distributed his pastries. Then he poured shots of bravery from his bottomless flask. When it became clear that the first responders were not responding, he did what he felt he had to do: he began pushing his customers over the edge. Many people were understandably resistant, but Charlie realized there was no other option. He snatched them one by one and tossed them over the side. But when the opportunity arose to follow suit, he responded, "No." He grabbed another customer from the terrified mob and made she take his spot.

Charles Joughin, high on adrenaline and drink, had taken it upon himself to load many lifeboats with dozens of terrified women and children, all of whom were reluctant to leave their husbands and fathers behind. The inebriated baker then defied gravity and basic intoxication norms by crawling over the side and scampered all the way to what must have felt like the top of the world. He rode the ruined ruins all the way down, flask in hand, waiting until the very last second before stepping from his perch into the 28-degree water.

He should have died, just like everyone else who did not make it to a lifeboat. But he did not. They said that the alcohol was what kept him alive, diluting his blood enough to prevent hypothermia.

If James Cameron had let Leonardo DiCaprio drink a few sips of whiskey, his character may have survived that awful night and grown old with Kate Winslet. Of all, there was no happy ending for Jack and Rose, or the 1,500 genuine individuals who died on their trip to New York City. Charles Joughin was not among them because the bar was open and unprotected.

Among all the horrible facts to focus on, I consider the conditions at the moment of the sinking. No wind. No waves. There is no movement. According to all accounts, the Atlantic was flat when the big ship sank. Flat and black, like a duck pond—a dark mirror with no reflections. How dreadful for the skipper, who was aware he was driving the ship too fast?

Seven years after Leonardo DiCaprio went to the bottom of James Cameron's sea, the Discovery Channel asked me to host a documentary called Deadliest Catch.

"It's not really 'on brand,'" they informed me. "It will never make it to series. But at least you won't have to crawl through sewers!"

I'm skeptical when network execs tell me what their "brand" is. It seems to me that your "brand" should be whatever your viewers are willing to watch. But I was grateful for the work and excited to visit Alaska.

"Why are you calling it Deadliest Catch?"

"Crab fishing is dangerous," the CEOs explained. "Plus it's a snappy title."

I arrived in Dutch Harbor several days after Thanksgiving. The trip had carried me from San Francisco to Seattle, which was pleasant; Seattle to Anchorage, which was also pleasant; and finally over the wide Bering Sea to Dutch Harbor, which was unpleasant. Not nice at all.

Technically, I suppose it was turbulence, but not the kind I had encountered in the lower forty-eight. It was a type of turbulence particular to islands with high hills around tiny runways buffeted by frequent crosswinds. It snapped the overhead compartments open. It sent a beverage cart careening down the aisle.

A hundred feet before landing, our pilot aborted and flew to Cold Bay, where he landed on a runway built for the space shuttle. We spent 24 hours there waiting for the weather to clear, eating stale snacks from vending machines in the deserted airport.

When I eventually arrived in Dutch, I went straight to the docks, where the film crew was preparing to board a crab boat. Was this the Fierce Allegiance? The maverick? The Bountiful? I can't remember. I do recall the rain blowing sideways and turning to sleet as I hopped on. Remember, it was 2004, and all I knew was that I'd be anchoring a documentary about crab fishing. I had no idea what the show would become. Nobody knew. But the filmmaker wanted footage of me baiting the big 800-pound pots and conversing with the crew to give the viewer an idea of how crab boats operated on the broad ocean. It was an unusual job to play: part host, half greenhorn, and part reporter—a bizarre combination that left the deckhands perplexed as to my true purpose on their boat. I shared a sense of bewilderment.

Things became sporty about twenty miles outside of Dutch. Green water rolled over the bow as we sank through wave after wave in twelve-foot swells. The wind increased up, I vomited, and the waves grew larger—but the labor never stopped. In the wheelhouse, the captain had a lit cigarette in each hand while one dangled from his mouth. He resembled a human chimney. The big, 800-pound pots on deck slid back and forth as the surf rose up around us.

I lived, and by Christmas, I had become accustomed to the snotgreen sea. By New Year's Day, my scrotum had returned to normal. It could have stayed that way except for the events of January 15, when the weather did something truly terrible.

The boat that sank that day was dubbed the Big Valley. She slipped beneath the surface as I was sleeping in the hotel. Conditions weren't to blame. In fact, when the ship left port, the Bering Sea was flat and black, like a duck pond—a dark mirror without a reflection. Perhaps it is why the captain left with so many pots. Way too many. However, the Bering Sea is an unpredictable environment, and when the wind picked up, the Big Valley became unstable. A deadly trap. Six men died as a result, 70 miles off St. Paul Island.

How awful must it have been to be slowly drawn beneath the surface? How bad for the captain, who knew his boat was carrying too much weight?

Deadliest Catch had lived up to its moniker, I suppose, but in ways we hadn't expected or desired. Ways that still bother me now.

Chapter 4: ON THE IMPORTANCE OF BETTER DRIVING

In May 1932, a sixty-one-year-old handyman called John Thompson was tinkering in his garage when he had a eureka moment—a self-centered concept that would almost completely eliminate bad driving. Bad driving was rampant back then, and automakers in the United States had no idea what to do about it. However, Thompson believed that the difficulty was caused by the impediments they met, notably sunken gullies, complicated curves, and flat horizontal surfaces.

Six months later, he had a dazzling prototype in his garage, ready to go. Six months later, Patent No. 1,080,080 arrived in the US mail, granting him exclusive ownership of the technology that would almost eliminate bad driving. All he needed was for someone to mass-produce it.

After two years of "no," John became discouraged. He'd never attempted to sell anything before, and the rejections were disheartening. He delivered his last pitch in a conference room packed with engineers at a manufacturing site in Oregon.

Later that evening, while bellying up to the bar, John was staring at the schematics on the wrinkled pages of his useless patent when a man with white teeth and flawless hair approached him.

"Don't take it too hard, pal. "A 'no' is simply a 'yes' to another question!"

"Spare me the platitudes," John stated. "I understand what 'no' means. "I hear it every day."

The man's name was Henry. He smiled, pulled up a stool, and ordered another round of drinks. "What exactly are you trying to sell?"

John handed Henry the patent. Henry didn't comprehend every aspect, but he saw the value of better driving. He offered to purchase one more round. He then offered to buy John's concept for a little sum of money. John agreed, and then everything occurred very quickly.

Henry returned to the corporation that had just rejected John's offer and requested to see the president, Eugene Clark. "Oh, no," the secretary replied. "Not without an appointment."

But Clark's secretary didn't realize that a "no" was simply a "yes" to another query. Henry smiled charmingly and showed her the patent he had purchased. "This idea is going to eliminate driver error," stated the politician. "I can show it to a competitor, but wouldn't you rather show it to the boss yourself?"

The secretary examined the patent. She, like Henry, did not comprehend all of the technicalities but saw the need of better driving.

"Mr. Clark, I just heard from General Motors." They want millions of these items. Your engineers claim it can't be done. Should I get someone else to attempt it, or do you want to give it another shot?"

Clark took up the phone and beckoned his engineers back into the conference room. Once again, the engineers evaluated the prototype and replied, "No." They cited the practical limitations of a cold steel forge and the numerous obstacles of scaling a product of this size. However, the engineers did not grasp that a "no" was simply a "yes" to another inquiry. At that moment, Henry flew to Detroit to urge General Motors to make a large order for a million gadgets that did not yet exist.

You can guess what came next. Henry met with the president of

General Motors and persuaded him to test the prototype. Driver performance improved considerably, and General Motors offered to purchase Henry's innovation. But this time, Henry responded "No." Henry had no intention of selling his driving method to just anyone. He wants to license it to everyone.

Eventually, General Motors ordered millions. Next, there's Chrysler. Then Ford. Next comes the Department of Defense. Henry's unique invention ended up in every new vehicle on American roads. Henry's bank account? That amounted to $65 million in today's dollars. And what about John Thompson?

He got screwed.

There truly isn't any way to describe it. The aging handyman had been correct all along. He was the one who replaced the bothersome gullies with a distinctive, tapered cruciform. He was the one who looked at those horizontal planes and saw what an inventive conical helix could accomplish. His revolutionary Self-Centering Drive System solved the long-standing problem of over-torqueing by automatically ejecting drivers before they could cause major damage. Not human drivers. Mechanical drivers. That discovery significantly boosted the pace and productivity of American production lines. However, the innovation was not named after the individual who conceived or designed it. It was called for the man who purchased and sold it multiple times.

A salesperson who understood that a "no" was only a "yes" to another query.

Henry's last name is still associated with the screw that made him wealthy and the screwdriver that made him renowned. Phillips.

Over the years, I've had the opportunity to speak on behalf of some very outstanding firms, including Ford, Caterpillar, Discovery, Hewlett-Packard, and Motorola, to name a few. I was also selling a range of dubious products on the QVC cable shopping channel between 3:00 and 6:00 a.m.

In 1990, QVC was having trouble attracting show hosts. Experienced salespeople were uncomfortable on television. Experienced TV people were hesitant to offer their products. That was the audition, and for reasons that would probably require a psychiatrist to untangle, I was able to go on and on about the qualities and benefits of a Dixon Ticonderoga no. 2. I was employed and assigned to the graveyard shift for the three-month, nocturnal crucible known as "the probationary period."

In retrospect, it was an excellent way to learn: three hours of live television with no script. With no prompter, no delays, and almost no supervision. Marty, a former host and producer, was sleeping at his desk while I was working. For me, it was a true baptism by fire, partly because I'd never appeared on television before and partly because there was no formal training program.

On my first shift, I arrived on set at precisely 3:00 a.m. Four robotic cameras confronted me, controlled by a crew of operators concealed behind a smoked glass pane twenty yards distant. That specific hour was titled Ideas for Your Home. What kind of house? It was difficult to say, considering the things I had been expected to sell. Every five minutes or so, a stagehand would bring me a new item, such as the Amcor negative ion generator, a hand-painted Hummel figurine, the first cordless phone I'd ever seen, or the first Karaoke machine.

I started with a Katsak, a paper shopping bag wrapped with Mylar that is said to generate a "crinkling" sound that cats find "irresistible." Yes, this is real. It's available online. You can actually watch me try to sell this item on YouTube for ten minutes, talking about the Katsak.

No one purchased any.

They then brought me a lava lamp, which I tried to open in the air to see whether there was any lava within. There wasn't. Nobody bought any of those, either.

Then they brought me the Healthteam Infrared Pain Reliever. It resembled a small flashlight with a cord attached. It costs $29.99 and claims to "relieve arthritic pain with healing infrared light when applied directly to the troubled area."

With eight minutes remaining on the clock and no coherent thought in my head, I looked into the camera and stated, "Folks, I'll be honest with you: I have no idea what this thing is or how it works. I'm suspicious of infrared light's therapeutic power. If you have one of these items, call the 800 number displayed on the screen. Ask for Marty. He'll put you on air. Maybe you can tell me whether it really works."

Ten seconds later, something extraordinary occurred. Someone called in. Carol, a pleasant person, described exactly what the device worked and informed me she was extremely happy with hers. She also said I had lovely eyes. After that, things became weirder but more entertaining.

Years later, when narrating a nature documentary, I discovered that when attacked by larger, stronger wolves, juvenile wolves will occasionally roll onto their backs, exposing their bellies. According to my physician, this is the same reason my dog pees on me when I return home: he "respects my authority." I am not sure I buy that. In fact, I'm rather certain Freddy is just incontinent. But I believe there are multiple ways to sell anything. For me, the secret was to reveal my fragility on camera and stop pretending to know more than I did. To adopt my own submissive position.

Chapter 5: NO POLITE WAY TO PUT IT

George was horny. Sorry for being impolite, but there isn't a polite way to say it. He hadn't seen Elizabeth in weeks, and he missed her with the intensity of a thousand suns.

"Excuse me, sir, but a letter has arrived."

George leapt from his chair and dashed to the doorway. "Hand it over, my good man, with all due speed."

The courier complied. George locked the door behind him. With shaky hands, he opened the letter. The sight of her penmanship made his heart quicken. The scent of her perfume floated off the page, leaving him dizzy and breathless.

"Oh, my gallant champion," it said. "Oh, how I miss you. If only we could be together for a few hours. "If only I could take 'Tomboy' for a quick ride with you behind me."

George swallowed hard and gripped the page with his free hand. By God, his woman could turn a phrase!

The second time went better. It always was. George read more carefully now, with all the patience he could summon. He relished each phrase, pausing between paragraphs to completely absorb the imagery his wife had so deftly conjured. When he was finished, he wiped the sweat from his brow and attempted to return the favor.

"Good morning, my rosebud," he wrote. " 'Little John' has been making regular and sincere requests for his bunkey for a very long time, and this morning, he appears more insistent than ever. I, too, desire to be in the saddle behind you, clutching on for dear life! And, yes, I know exactly where I'd kiss someone if I were with her tonight."

Two weeks later, his letter arrived in Monroe, Michigan. The butler delivered it to the boudoir. Elizabeth swallowed his words just as he had devoured hers. Hungrily. Greedily. In other words, George and Elizabeth were sexting in a Victorian style.

Sorry for being impolite, but there isn't a nicer way to say it. Their letters were the nineteenth-century equivalent of nude selfies, brimming with double meanings that would have made Anthony Weiner blush. There were phrases like "long, extended gallops" and "riding under the crupper."

True, George was a well-known equestrian, but no one would have mistaken the subject. Of course no one did. George was more than simply a hot husband; he was also a thoughtless husband.

Elizabeth's letters were once stolen. They made an appearance in the Richmond Gazette. Soon, the entire country was reading about "Little John," the pleasures of riding "Tomboy," and that "soft place upon someone's carpet," in need of a loving touch.

One can only image how Elizabeth felt when her words appeared in print. Nonetheless, she overcame the scandal. People eventually forgot all about it. Likewise, they overlooked her husband's other flaws. They forgot about his impulsive personality. They forgot about his need to always be the center of attention. By the time she died at the age of ninety, she had single-handedly transformed George's reputation—not from that of a reckless husband who'd notoriously embarrassed his wife, but from that of a distinguished commander who'd carelessly slaughtered his own soldiers.

In the film, George dies with his boots on, battling valiantly till the very end. In reality, no one knows. Three days after the smoke cleared, his body was discovered nude, burned, bloated, and covered with flies. Some claimed a finger was severed and taken as a souvenir. Some reported he appeared to be smiling (as the dead frequently do), while others claimed an arrow had been (excuse me) driven into his rectum, pushed through his intestines, and into his "Little John," putting his corpse in a condition of constant readiness even as it putrefied under the blue Montana sky.

Sorry for being impolite, but there isn't a nicer way to say it. Some of George's soldiers were skinned alive. Others were disassembled and rearranged on the ground. President Ulysses S. Grant described the entire episode as "an abominable, totally unnecessary slaughter caused by the stupidity and rashness of a vain, corkheaded fool."

Although not a happy conclusion for the impatient Boy General, he left a far better legacy than he deserved—a blushing bride named Elizabeth Custer, a best-selling author.

I was thinking about Custer not long ago, at Grumpy's, after narrating a couple more episodes of How the Universe Works for my Science Channel friends. The only ambiguity appears to be the precise method of my untimely end. What will it be? Is there a gigantic black hole? A collision between two neutron stars? A supernova? A comet? An asteroid? What about gamma rays?

Is it any surprise that after a long day of this, I usually wind up at Grumpy's?

On that particular day, I had introduced my audience to the concept of "strangelets"—killer particles that "zombify" matter, whatever that term means. I wasn't blasé about it.

Once, I was asked to rerecord a passage that mentioned the total number of galaxies in the universe. I had previously stated, in a crisp, well-modulated baritone, that there were "approximately one hundred billion galaxies in the known universe."

I recall thinking, "Damn, that's a lot of galaxies"—and, as a narrator of some experience, I instilled the material with what I considered was an acceptable amount of conviction and seriousness.

A week later, I was called back to the booth. A new method of monitoring the cosmos caused astronomers to revise the number of galaxies in the known universe from a hundred billion to two trillion. In one week, we discovered another two thousand billion galaxies. But as I reread the new copy, I was struck by the incontrovertible reality that I sound just as convinced when I'm right as when I'm wrong.

It's difficult to say in these uncertain times. But there are no warriors among my unquestionably large audience, waiting to accompany me into combat. Custer had six hundred soldiers behind him—the whole 7th Regiment—hanging on his every word. I can't help but wonder: How assured did Custer sound, under a great, blue Montana sky, as he led his soldiers into that valley of death?

Unfortunately, there was no recording studio to call Custer back to. There were no do-overs for him or his guys. Just a knife, an arrow, and a tomahawk.

That much I am certain of.

Chapter 6: A PATIENT MAN

John was a patient man. His attraction to Peggy had been instantaneous and profound; their courtship, a whirlwind of barely suppressed passion. And now, as John stood at the altar, watching the object of his affection walk slowly toward him, his thoughts were those of a man whose patience was finally about to pay off.

As Peggy drew ever closer and the organ heralded the coming of the bride, John recalled the day he'd proposed. At first Peggy had demurred. She'd said she'd "think about it tomorrow." But John was persistent as well as patient, and eventually she said "Yes." How happy he had been. How relieved. He knew that she had broken off all those engagements. But now here they were: Peggy in her wedding gown and John in his tuxedo, standing just a few feet apart.

The ceremony was a blur. Scriptures were quoted, songs were sung, the minister spoke sacred words, and all of Atlanta's society bore witness. Then the tricky part came.

John glanced out at the faces of those assembled in the crowded church and held his breath. He knew that several of Peggy's previous suitors were in attendance. Would they object? What would he do if they did?

The moment passed. John exhaled, slowly. And when the minister asked the groom if he would "love, honor, and cherish Peggy from this day forward," John stared into the face of his true love and said the only thing that he could say: nothing. Because the preacher was not talking to John. The preacher was talking to John's best friend, a man named Berrien Upshaw—Red to his friends. Today, Red was the man that Peggy was marrying.

John had numerous objections, but he was unwilling to "forever hold his peace," thus he had no intention of "speaking now." He went on with his idea instead. He smiled. He gave Red the wedding band and applauded as his best buddy wedded the love of his life.

The ensuing days, weeks, and months were difficult for John. He realized his genuine love was in the arms of another man. But John couldn't quite blame Peggy. Red was a charmer. He looked like a movie star. John Marsh, on the other hand, was a soft-spoken public relations professional who dabbled in journalism. As Peggy had told John when she broke their engagement, along with his heart, "Life is under no obligation to give us what we expect."

Indeed.

However, when it came to expectations, John had an advantage over Red and Peggy. He knew them. He knew them better than they did themselves or one another.

John was aware that Red expected a submissive and willing wife. He knew Peggy anticipated a patient and caring husband.

He would be more likely to bash his blushing bride. Peggy would never accept that.

After two months, Red had had enough of the feisty woman who couldn't stop speaking her mind. When she showed him a little too much sass, he showed her the back of his hand—and that was it. Peggy left, and John was waiting to pick up the pieces. He eventually proposed again. Peggy said she'd think about it tomorrow.

John smiled and replied, "I heard that one yesterday." Peggy smiled back and answered "Yes" right away. They lived happily ever after.

Sadly, "ever after" would only endure 24 years. Peggy was killed by a drunk driver when she was only forty-eight. However, during her time with John, she discovered not just genuine love, but also her own voice. With John's support, Peggy began writing. She discussed love and passion, pride and prejudice, war and death, hope, and all in between. Some believe she wrote the account of her own life.

Peggy never verified this. However, the most renowned character she created was a strong-willed southern belle: Pansy, a beautiful socialite whom every man desired to marry. Peggy insisted that Pansy had nothing to do with her.

Whatever the truth was, the publishers adored Peggy's manuscript. They did make one alteration to the 1,037-page work, which eventually won the Pulitzer Prize and sold 30 million copies. They thought the name "Pansy" was too weak for the fiery persona Peggy had created out of thin air—and John convinced Peggy that the publishers were correct.

In real life, this is exactly what happened. A handsome bootlegger named Red Upshaw simply didn't care—while an average Joe named John Marsh was assured that tomorrow would be another day.

I remember a television commercial that aired during Baltimore Orioles home games. It was intended for an amusement park in Ocean City, Maryland. According to the announcer, a visit there would be "the time of my life." At the time, I had lived for roughly nine years. For the most part, I was pleased with how things were going. Then I spotted the wild mouse.

The Wild Mouse was a massive roller coaster that threatened to spring from our black-and-white television and slam into the wall of our small den. I'd never seen anything like them before—a parade of gadgets designed solely for entertainment. I recall the camera focusing in on a child around my age. He was strapped into the Wild Mouse next to a beautiful girl, his eagerness bordering on ecstasy. I was transfixed.

"Hey, Peggy, check out these ding-a-lings on TV. I think they'll puke on each other."

My parents sat on the sofa behind me. "Oh, those poor children," Mom commented. "Why would anyone stand in line all day just to get vomited on?"

"Obviously, Peggy, those youngsters are crazy. "Look at them."

I looked through the sea of happy faces for signs of ignorance or nausea.

"Isn't it sad, John, how some children need machines to have fun?"

"It certainly is, Peg. "It certainly is."

Later, another commercial surfaced, this time promoting the film Willie Wonka and the Chocolate Factory. According to the announcer, the picture playing at the Senator was "a thrilling film for the whole family…a must-see event!". I'd never been to the Senator, or any other movie theater. I was mesmerized.

"Tell me something, Peggy. Why would anyone want to watch the movie if they could read the book instead? "Books are much more interesting."

"Well, John, from what I hear, movies are for children who can't read well. "Isn't that sad?"

"It certainly is, Peg. "It certainly is."

In 1971, we didn't have enough money for amusement parks or "must-see" attractions. But I never felt awful about missing such events. I was too busy feeling terrible for those who had to go through things.

My father groaned and spoke with a melancholy tone. "Look, son, Bobby's mother does not know how to cook. It's not her fault they can't eat normal meals. Then I gently told my mother, "Peg, maybe you should call Mrs. Price and give her the recipe for your meat loaf casserole."

"Of course, John." That poor guy needs a homemade dinner."

"He certainly does, Peg. "He certainly does."

It was an unusual kind of snobbery to develop at such a young age—sympathy for the better fortunate—but that is exactly what my parents instilled. They manipulated jealousy into pity.

One Sunday after church, our neighbors stopped by with a slideshow of images from their most recent family vacation, which included Yellowstone and Yosemite. The Brannigans stayed for several hours, telling stories about Indians, geysers, and wild bears. My brothers and I were spellbound.

My mother dabbed her tears with a Kleenex, like a one-person Greek chorus. "Gosh, John, can you imagine flying all the way across the country just to take a walk in the woods?"

"No, honey, I certainly can't. However, not everyone has a forest in their backyard!"

"That is a good point, John. "Very good point."

Later, when I was less gullible (and TV advertising were more compelling), a new parenting style emerged, incorporating terms like "No!" and "Because I said so!" But when I started sixth grade, I was well aware that movie theaters were for the uneducated, vacations for the unimaginative, and home delivery for lazy moms who couldn't cook. Amusement parks were probably fine if you didn't mind standing in line all day for the opportunity to vomit all over your pals.

Chapter 7: ANOTHER TORTURED ARTIST

Back in the 1970s, before the world knew him by a single name, a bruised child looked into an unforgiving mirror and saw his reflection: a split lip, a swollen jaw, and a black eye. severe, but not as severe as the words that came with the beating: "Look in that mirror, boy." Your lips are too large for your mouth, your nose is too flat for your face, and your skin is not the same as your brothers'.

In his mother's makeup cabinet, the boy discovered a solution: a glass jar containing white powder. He opened it, dusted some powder into his hands, and started rubbing it on his face, hurting as he went. His scars were still raw, courtesy of the man who would not accept a single error onstage or in rehearsal. However, the boy in the mirror noticed that his complexion gradually lightened. Would it be enough to calm his aggressive and unpredictable father?

As the boy's talent grew increasingly apparent, such questions became less and less significant. By the end of the 1970s, the boy had become famous. By the 1980s, he was a national sensation. By the 1990s, he was a global phenomenon. By the turn of the century, he was unquestionably the King of Pop. Despite his notoriety, he never ceased fretting about the color of his skin. Even when his legacy was well established. Even when his personal life started to disintegrate. Even when his odd friendship with a fourteen-year-old youngster resulted in controversy and a legal drama.

Even in the weight of depression and addiction, the King of Pop kept his actual complexion hidden until the day he died, alone in his bed.

If all of this seems faintly similar, it's because you've heard the story of another wounded youngster who stood before another merciless mirror—two decades later, in the 1970s—and studied his reflection.

He had a split lip, swelling jaw, and black eye. severe, but not as severe as the comments that came with the beating: "Look at yourself, boy.

It's interesting how history tends to repeat itself. He, too, was born with a different skin tone than his brothers. He, too, was reared by a violent, unpredictable father who abused his talent at every opportunity. If you Google his name, you can see the evidence for yourself: a new nose, a new chin, new lips, new eyelids, another new nose, new cheekbones, new hair, another new nose, new brows, new eyelashes, one more new nose—and, through it all, a complexion that got lighter and lighter until the day he died alone in his bed.

It's tempting to blame the father for the son's problems, and perhaps we should. By all accounts, Joseph Jackson did a serious damage on the talented, deeply disturbed artist we know as Michael.

Johann, like Joseph, forced his son to perform and rehearse every day of his early life. Like Joseph, Johann relied on his son to pay the expenses. A son with a skin that he thought was too dark.

Fortunately, the most anguished artist of all time had no idea that his music would end up on Hitler's playlist—a little blessing, maybe, for the abused youngster who was never happy in his own skin. The lonely bachelor who never discovered his Immortal Beloved. The renowned composer who became deaf at the height of his abilities but continued to create—even though he couldn't hear the ovation his numerous masterpieces elicited. Beethoven, sometimes known as the "King of Pop," faced significant challenges.

The other day, as I flipped through the channels on the television, Beethoven sprang to me. It was a rainy Sunday in San Francisco, and I'd just discovered Steven Spielberg's Band of Brothers.

Band of Brothers, like Caddyshack, Jaws, and The Shawshank Redemption, is a film I can't stop watching—and the sequence I discovered on this rainy Sunday is my favorite moment in the entire series.

The sequence begins in the aftermath of an Allied onslaught, with the elderly, shell-shocked people of a bombed-out German village shuffling like zombies through the rubble of their neighborhood, retrieving their broken goods from vast piles of debris. As a small group of American GIs observes the scene, we hear what could be the finest piece of music ever composed: Beethoven's Opus 131's sixth movement. It's more than just a soundtrack; it's an integral component of the scenario.

"All you need is a little Mozart," another GI says.

At this point, Lieutenant Lewis Nixon, played beautifully by Ron Livingston (the guy from Office Space), corrects the soldier with two sentences delivered with the ideal blend of authority and world-weary awe.

"That's not Mozart," he explains. "That's Beethoven."

Why do I enjoy this scene so much? In part, I believe it is the juxtaposition of beauty and ruin. When placed so close together, each accentuates the other. The combo makes me cry every time I see it. I sympathize with German folks. But I feel completely with the GI who confuses Mozart and Beethoven. As someone who makes public mistakes on a regular basis, I understand how embarrassing it is to be corrected on camera. Indeed, when it comes to getting corrected, you could call myself an expert.

On Dirty Jobs, I received corrections from hundreds of different managers in every possible circumstance. As the perpetual newcomer, I was corrected about windmills and oil derricks, coal mines and construction sites, frack tanks, pig farms, slime lines, and timber mills. Today, I have a podcast that delves into history and biography, as well as a Facebook group full of individuals determined to keep me accountable.

Take my cantankerous field producer, David Barsky. Barsky, like my father, is incapable of listening to a story if one or more facts appear to be out of place. In fact, a few chapters into this book, Barsky will read about Mel Brooks and phone me right away, guaranteed.

"Hey, genius," he'll say. "The 'vinyl' record you cited could not have been on vinyl. It was shellac. It had to be, because vinyl was not used for record production in 1944." This will be the high point of Barsky's week.

My father, a former history teacher, will immediately phone to inquire how I knew Custer's remains had been raped in the manner described. "You don't know that!" he'll exclaim. "Experts continue to fight about it!! Just because people say something is true does not make it so!!!" Those exclamation marks will bounce off satellites and pierce my ears like arrows.

My mother is also a hopeless corrector—of the sorry type. At least she pretends to be.

"Oh, Michael," she will say. "I apologize, but there is a double negative at the top of this section. You stated, 'I can't not watch.' Sorry, Mike; it's a terrific story, but I assumed you'd be interested."

Personally, I do not mind being corrected, even when I am accurate. It's good to know that others are paying attention. However, when I am corrected, I prefer it to be in the style of Lieutenant Dixon. He did not chastise the GI for mixing Mozart with Beethoven. He was neither arrogant, pompous, or disappointed. His words contained no apologies. In fact, if you watch the scene on YouTube, you'll notice he barely looks at the individual he's correcting. He simply resolves the situation while remaining focused on Beethoven's final few measures.

By the way, I ran into Ron Livingston a few years ago in Los Angeles. He was eating sushi with several buddies at Katsu-Ya, which is located in a strip mall off Ventura Boulevard. I was seated a few tables away with my high school friend Chuck. I've never approached a celebrity in my life, let alone one with a mouthful of fish. But I couldn't control myself. I approached Ron's table and stood quietly, making things awkward, until he returned my look.

For a second, I feared he was going to leave me hanging. But he did not. Lieutenant Dixon devoured his fish, sipped his beer, and said exactly what I expected him to say: "That's not Mozart. "That is Beethoven."

The point is that the following story contains no mistakes. But if you locate one, please let me know on my Facebook page. And while you're there, say hello to my father!!!

Chapter 8: SIZE MATTERS

Bill had a large one, no doubt about it, but Craig's was much bigger. Craig had more inches, albeit not by much. So Bill made a few tweaks. But Bill had one last trick up his sleeve. When the measuring was finished, one of these men could confidently claim to have the world's largest erection.

When it comes to New York City architecture, size does important.

Their collaboration had been legendary. Bill was the artist—a superb architect who lacked personality. Craig was the epitome of a businessman: gorgeous, witty, and driven. They had formed an ideal team. Craig secured all high-profile commissions. Bill designed the stunning, ground-breaking structures that made them both wealthy.

Unfortunately, their egos rose alongside their bank accounts. Craig was an outstanding architect in his own right. He didn't appreciate the continuous newspaper pieces praising Bill's "artistic genius." Bill, for his part, despised being viewed as a boardroom lightweight incapable of handling major transactions. He despised the way clients looked at Craig when they talked about finances.

Eventually, the artist and the businessman split up in a very public, very acrimonious divorce. Then, as fate would have it, each received the commission of a lifetime.

A business tycoon approached Bill in 1928, asking him to create the world's tallest building. Bill agreed and submitted blueprints for an 809-foot-tall tower in midtown Manhattan.

Craig then agreed to design the Bank of Manhattan Trust Building on

Wall Street. His concept called for the construction of an 840-foot-tall tower.

When Bill saw Craig's design was 31 feet taller than his, he promptly added two stories to his blueprint. Craig responded by adding another floor to his. Bill followed suit.

When the final blueprints were approved, everyone felt the battle was over: Bill's Midtown tower would be the world's highest building. Craig's Tower on Wall Street would be a close second. But a man like Craig could never be second banana, especially to his ex-partner. The towers were built in 1930. Craig then revealed his secret weapon: the massive tip, dubbed the "Lantern," combined with a flagpole that raised 40 Wall Street to 927 feet, two feet higher than Bill's Midtown tower. Craig was overjoyed that 40 Wall Street was now the tallest building in the world.

Because a man like Bill would not be second banana—especially since his old colleague was the man in the top place.

So, on May 22—only thirty days after Craig claimed the world's largest erection—Bill took a private elevator to the seventy-first floor of his Midtown masterpiece. He peered six miles south to see his former partner's rising giant. He then gave the signal.

Of course, erections are unpredictable. Size is important, but it is not the primary factor in determining contentment. The businessman who had hired Bill to build what he called "a monument to myself" was now refusing to pay him the entire commission.

Bill brought the tycoon to court. Eventually, he received his money. However, in those elegant days of boater hats and pocket fobs, a lawsuit was considered an ungentlemanly manner to conduct business.

Unlike Bill the Artist, Craig the Businessman was highly compensated for his work at 40 Wall Street. His building is no longer the world's second tallest, third, fifth, or twenty-fifth. But it's worth noting that, for one magnificent month in the spring of 1930, no one had a bigger one than H. Craig Severance—an architect who valued the art of the transaction over the artistry of his chosen trade.

Something for the current owner to think about. Another New York builder who has occasionally reflected on the relevance of size. A man whose surname currently adorns the exterior of 40 Wall Street in large gold letters. Huge letters. Perhaps the biggest letters in the entire globe!

They may not be the biggest, but they are definitely huge.

In terms of erections, you know the saying: if it's not one thing, it's your mother.

In this case, my own. Peggy Rowe's book, About My Mother, openly discusses her passion for horses. My grandma told me that she frequently skipped meals and school to care for the ponies she was in charge of. Little changed after she married my father and had three sons. Our major goal, as far as we could tell, was to clean up the countless piles of steaming manure that covered the little field back our farmhouse while she ensured that the horses were fed, watered, exercised, brushed, fed some more, brushed again, and nestled in for the evening. After that, she would occasionally feed her children, albeit with much less enthusiasm.

When I was twelve, my mother entered me into an equestrian competition at the Maryland State Fair. She was desperate to instill in me the same illness that had infected her, and resisting was fruitless. "Mom," I explained, "I don't want to ride English. "It's for girls."

"Stop being foolish, Michael. The best riders in the world ride English. "Any fool can grab the horn and gallop around on western tack like a drunken cowboy."

That sounded far better to me than the navy jacket (with black piping) that I had to wear with creamy spandex breeches, a blousy pirate shirt, and knee-high black boots. Worst of all was the helmet, a spherical bowl that was far too small for my already large skull, wrapped in silky black velvet and secured with an elastic chinstrap. I was so horrified by the item that I could only stand there while Mom attached it to my head.

I resembled a Pez dispenser on a pony. Tammy is the name of a pony.

The competition did not go well, and the humiliation remained, as it frequently does, and I am still suspicious of spandex, helmets, and females named Tammy.

Chic was led inside the stable and introduced to a pommel horse, a piece of gymnastic equipment whose name finally made sense. On the opposite side of the pommel horse, a mare in heat was waiting. Paid by Chic was prepared for the daily dance, having grown accustomed to it. The tumescence was humbling. The vagina was a brilliant blue container around the size of a breadbox. Consider a hot-water bottle with a sturdy cloth grip on the top. Dr. Christine handed me the gadget, a jar of lubricant, and a baby bottle.

"Go ahead," she replied. "Squeeze some lube into the artificial vagina."

"How much?" I asked.

"Can't have too much lube," she said. "Now go ahead and screw that baby bottle into the back end."

"I beg your pardon?" "I said."

"Plug the back end of the artificial vagina with the baby bottle so that the sperm has somewhere to go. "Just screw it in."

That was one of several sentences I'd never heard before. "The sooner the better," she added.

Paid by Chic had taken up a position of absolute preparedness on the pommel horse. His front legs were thrown over the side. His gaze was fixed on the mare just out of reach. His horsehood was surging aimlessly into midair.

"Okay," I said. "I'm ready."

I approached the engorged beast.

"Hold on, Champion. You wouldn't approach a horse in that condition without one of these. Last week, one of our best grooms was knocked unconscious."

I could only stand there, shocked, as she attached it to my skull. It didn't fit at all, just like the velvet monstrosity of my youth. But, once again, I was in compliance and ready to act.

Mom called to congratulate me only moments after the episode aired.

"Oh, Michael, you're very lucky! Paid by Chic is one of the best quarter horses alive! And you looked great in your small cycling helmet."

"Thank you, Mom." "The whole thing was humbling."

"Yes," she answered. "I imagine it was."

I didn't need to say that three minutes later, Paid by Chic humiliated me again with an encore performance. A performance that added to my baby bottle's white gold deposit. A performance worthy of the close-ups, slow pans, and artful fades that helped Dirty Jobs become the family-friendly show it is.

After all, she's my mother.

Chapter 9: CAN YOU BE THERE BY NINE?

Al sat on the back of a horse that wasn't his, drew an unloaded pistol, and shot an Apache who was not an Indian. The stuntman screamed and fell unconvincingly to the ground, as the director cried, "Cut!" Back to one, everyone! "Let us do it again!"

Al looked uneasily at his watch. 6:30 p.m. Not good. His audition was at nine a.m. the next day—St. George, Utah, was seven hours by road from Los Angeles—and Al didn't own a car.

"All right, everyone. Here we go. Ready? "And... action!"

Once again, Indians whooped and stormed, civilians shouted and scattered, and Al fired the shot, killing the same man for the tenth time that day. But suddenly, when the Apache who was not an Indian dropped on the ground, the director yelled, "Cut!" That's it, everyone! Check the call times for tomorrow!"

Al knew his call time: 3:00 p.m. Tight, but possible.

Five miles later, as the sun was starting to set, Al arrived at the highway. He dismounted, turned his horse back toward the stables, and slapped it on the rump. Horses always know where the stable is, especially around dinnertime. After that one vanished in a puff of dust, Al realized there was no turning back. He held his thumb out, and two hours later, an 18-wheeler eventually stopped.

Al got at the studio with two minutes to spare. He didn't appear like a man who had ridden a horse, caught a ride, and slept in an airport to audition for a position he was unlikely to get. He resembled Jonas Grumby, the smiling, bumbling, irritated guy he'd come to read about.

Al took another look at the lines he'd already remembered. He walked in the room. A slender kid wearing a goofy hat was waiting in front of a camera. Al shook the kid's hand and talked briefly about the scene. Then someone exclaimed, "Action!"

That was it. Magic. Nobody would ever look at Al and wonder where they had seen his face. Thanks to that audition and five decades of syndication, Al's face would be permanently imprinted on America's retina. Jonas Grumby would have more screen time than all of the actors Al had ever worked with combined.

So, when Al died in 1990, his ashes were scattered over the Pacific Ocean—a fitting send-off for the man who became synonymous not with the cowboys he'd so often portrayed or the Indians he'd so often shot, but with Jonas Grumby—the sailor whose name was changed after the show's pilot to the one you know now. The common title by which he was addressed every day for the rest of his life.

Alan Hale, Jr., a wonderful character actor who also happens to be a great character actor, embarked on a fatal journey.

Even though the real boss was a scrawny child with a goofy hat named Gilligan.

Alan Hale, Jr. never received an Oscar or an Emmy Award. He wasn't even nominated. But if Hollywood was in the business of character recognition, there'd be a trophy somewhere with his name on it. Perhaps even a statue. Because what Hale accomplished in 1964 was nothing short of extraordinary.

Imagine you're a middle-aged character actor. You're not wealthy. You have a wife and four children, all of whom rely on you.

Alan Hale, Jr. didn't care about celebrity. He believed in something far more noble, which Hollywood has never acknowledged and will most likely never recognize. He believed that a promise made was an unpaid debt, notably the commitment he'd made to care for and support his family. That's what makes him my hero.

My father first appeared onstage in 1975, as the lead in a production of Woody Allen's Don't Drink the Water. That persona was Walter Hollander, a middle-aged American tourist stuck with his family at the US Embassy in a fictitious country hidden behind the Iron Curtain.

I was transfixed. Who was this man inhabiting my father's body? Why was everyone laughing so hard—not only at what he said, but also at how he said it? Where was the no-nonsense teacher who'd come home every night and hover over me as I finished my homework? The strict taskmaster who woke me up every Saturday at 7:00 a.m. to split wood, mow the lawn, and shovel snow?

I recall a staging of Agatha Christie's Towards Zero. Dad played a Scottish inspector assigned to investigate a murder on a country estate. From the front row, I witnessed him confront the guilty individual with damning proof. I recognized the expression on his face right away: it was the same expression that accompanied countless earlier inspections, all of which were done in the house where I grew up.

"And whose muddy boots left this dirt on the carpet?"

"And who drank the last of the milk?"

"And whose socks are these, jammed into the sofa cushions?"

Such inquiries, addressed at my brothers and me, were invariably met with a raised eyebrow and some dramatic revelation: the soiled boot, empty milk carton, or stray sock, hoisted up for all to see: "A-ha!"

He had innate sleuthing abilities.

"We burn a hot fire here; it melts down all concealment!"

Sitting in the front row at the Dundalk Community Theater, I was convinced that his lyrics were aimed at me—and realizing that there was more to my father than I had believed made me wonder if there was more to me. Mom certainly seemed to believe so.

"Someday, Michael, you'll be the star of the show. "Exactly like your father."

If seeing my father was a luxury, working directly with him was an honor—a role you could say I was born for. In The Rainmaker, he played a sheriff who arrested me—for attempting to persuade desperate farmers that I could make rain amid a drought. That, too, was a really convincing portrayal.

Seven years after Dad made his Don't Drink the Water debut, I appeared in a production of the same play. Not in the same role—I was still too young to be a middle-aged American traveler. I auditioned for the role of Axel Magee, the foolish son of the US ambassador who has fallen in love with the lovely daughter of Walter Hollander, the character portrayed by my father.

The production took place in the Cockpit in the Court, one of Baltimore's most famous theater locations. I got butterflies on opening night. I recall the audience whispering on the other side of the curtain as the lights dimmed. But what I remember most vividly is Dad in the front row, laughing loudly in all the right places, undoubtedly wondering, "Who is this young man inhabiting my son's skin and getting all of these laughs?"

As I was writing my narrative about Alan Hale, Jr., my father was auditioning for a role in another production of Don't Drink the Water. He was in his mid-eighties and too experienced to play Walter Hollander.

Watching from the front row, I reflected on his varied roles throughout the years. All the rehearsals. He spent all of his time memorizing lines. I thought about the hospital where he volunteers two days a week, as well as the residents who look forward to his cheerful Meals on Wheels delivery every Monday.

After the show, he told me that things were not as simple as they used to be. However, as everyone who knows my father understands, "easy" was never the goal.

My guess is that Alan Hale, Jr. comprehended it as well.

Chapter 10: A FULL-FIGURED GAL

Libby was unquestionably a tall drink of water. A statuesque, full-figured woman who, in the words of Rodgers and Hammerstein, was "broad where a broad should be broad." Aside from her classic beauty, Libby had another trait that most men found irresistible—one that implied anything was possible with a lady like her.

Fred had conceived Libby twenty years ago—her mother had never been involved—but referring to Fred as a single father would be unfair. Fred loved his daughter as much as any parent could, but it was Gus who had raised her. And now Fred and Gus were attempting to arrange a marriage, exploring the world for a man who would elevate their girl.

For a moment, it appeared like the man would be Egypt's governor. Isma'il Pasha was gorgeous, charming, and definitely smitten with Libby. He said all the right things and offered to build her a magnificent home right at the entrance to the recently built Suez Canal. Fred was thrilled. Isma'il was obviously a Muslim, but Libby didn't care. She would wear the veil in public if it made him happy. But after two years of courtship, it was evident that Egypt was not the ideal environment for a lady like Libby.

Libby handled the rejection well, but Fred was devastated. He had wasted two years with Isma'il, and his little girl was not getting any younger. So Fred and Libby set ship for America, hoping to find a more acceptable mate.

Joe did not appear to be a natural fit. He was a thin man who had been labeled as "too scrawny for manual labor." He appeared childish in comparison to Libby. But Joe knew exactly what he wanted and how to achieve it. He had saved his money while working as a reporter for the St. Louis Post in Missouri. Eventually, he purchased the entire newspaper. He also bought the St. Louis Dispatch. Then he relocated to Manhattan and bought The World newspaper. Joe first saw Fred's daughter in New York. On the top page of his new newspaper, he announced that Libby would stay in the city with him.

Fred was thrilled. Obviously, Joe was a foreigner, but Libby didn't care. There was only one problem: when Fred informed Joe that he and Gus wanted to put Libby on a pedestal, he wasn't referring to a metaphor; he was referring to a real pedestal, one that would cost the city of New York at least $250,000. That's equivalent to $6 million now.

Philip and Eliza Bender were among the first to give, each giving 50 cents. Joe wrote their names, along with his gratitude, next to a photo of his lover. Their children also contributed, and Joe printed their names: "Anna, 25 cents; Frannie, 25 cents; Leonard, 10 cents; Frank, 15 cents; Alice, 10 cents; Ralph, 10 cents; Carri, 10 cents; Miss Nicey, 25 cents." Overall, the Benders were worth $2.30—and everyone read about it.

It's ironic that an immigrant, now well-known for the honors heaped upon him, is mostly forgotten for his greatest gift—the effort that kept our favorite woman right where she belongs. Thanks to thousands of New Yorkers, their pocket coins, and a guy named Joseph Pulitzer, we may argue that America once placed Liberty on a pedestal.

I had a pedestal once. I placed a pig on it. Google it. Go ahead—I will wait.

Are you back? Good. Let us proceed.

By 2005, Dirty Jobs was an undeniable success, but the network and I couldn't seem to agree on how to market it. They desired a typical marketing campaign with me at its center—a "working-class hero, earnestly attempting to master every blue-collar trade."

That made me extremely uncomfortable. Dirty Jobs was not considered a "earnest" show. It was not a show about me. It was a lighthearted tribute to ordinary folks who awoke clean and returned soiled. What I envisioned was a campaign in which ordinary people were not just included, but treated like celebrities. I pictured them in their work attire, as they appeared on the show, arriving in limos at a star-studded "red carpet" premiere, surrounded by cameras and greeted by throngs of enthusiastic fans.

Barsky, my intrepid field producer and grime partner, requested a campaign featuring me covered in "feces from every species" (a reoccurring subject in Season One). Barsky, a realism aficionado, also recommended a campaign including personal photos of me with each of the barnyard animals I'd artificially inseminated in my continued efforts to demystify animal husbandry.

All of these concepts had one thing in common: they were non-starters. As a result, we got stranded. Fortunately, my lawyer was on the case.

I do not have an agency, manager, or PR. I have a Mary. Her coworkers refer to her as the Irish Hammer.

Mary Sullivan is her full name. She was a biology major who one day chose to pursue a career in law. I am pleased she did. Mary had Farrah Fawcett's hair and Albert Einstein's brain, and when I learned the latter was larger than the former, I began asking her advice on everything.

Mary had heard of the "working-class hero" campaign already. She had snorted gracefully and called my boss. "Mike isn't a hero," she had stated. "He isn't the star of the show. He's not even the host. His employment requires him to stay out of the spotlight. His role is to shine the spotlight. My job is to prevent him from becoming an asshole. Or worse, from like one.

Candor is a scarce commodity in Hollywood. Charm is also an important factor. The Irish Hammer has both in spades, therefore the network has backed off. But we were back at square one with the promotion, and time was running out.

"What do you think I should do?" I asked Mary. "We need to film something this week."

Without looking up from her desk, the Irish Hammer asked, "What about the pig?"

"What pig?"

"The pig in the show open."

Every episode of Dirty Jobs begins with a shot of me hauling a 200-pound swine from a barn to a pig corral. (Incidentally, the pig appeared to have an erection, which was not spotted until viewers began to send in queries, but that's a story for another day.)

"I'm not sure I understand," I informed Mary. "You want to make a pig the star of the show?

"More like the mascot," she explained. "A metaphor for hard work."

"But pigs don't work hard," I explained. "Unless truffle hunting counts."

The Irish Hammer stared at me in the same manner that a wise person would consider a fool.

"Do you know what a metaphor is?"

"I think so."

"Have you ever cleaned a pig pen?"

"Several," I answered.

"Was it difficult?"

"Yes."

"Was it pleasant?"

"No."

"All well then. If you want to recognize people who undertake difficult, unpleasant professions without appearing sincere or self-centered, elevate the pig. Viewers are not stupid. They will figure it out. And you won't come off looking like an asshole."

Do you see what I mean? Don't let Farrah Fawcett's hair deceive you.

The next day, we scheduled a three-hundred-pound sow for an interesting picture. She was brought to Hollywood from a farm in the Central Valley, and she arrived at the soundstage early, eager for her big moment. She was a perfect pig, straight from the animal equivalent of Central Casting: pink, with gray markings and a lovely personality. Like Wilbur from Charlotte's Web, but more grown up. I called her "Rhonda."

Looking back, putting a pig on a pedestal was probably the smartest thing I've ever done. It not only made Rhonda famous, but it also established me as an atypical show host. One whose principal task was to appear more like a guest than a host. Also, whenever possible, avoid acting like an asshole. Opinions differ on the extent to which I succeeded, but I must have done something right because Mary Sullivan eventually consented to quit her firm and partner with me, for which I am always thankful. And as for Rhonda, a poster of her currently hangs at the Irish Hammer office. Rhonda, like Libby, welcomes visitors to mikeroweWORKS from her perch, keeping me honest and a little dirty.

Chapter 11: THE ORPHAN HERO

She was an orphan living on the frigid streets of a terrible town, doing whatever she needed to do to survive. Unlike other runaways, she did not flee when they approached her. In reality, she greeted them with a puzzled smile, recognizing their government van for what it was: a warm refuge on a cold evening. She got inside.

Orphans make excellent protagonists, as is well known. Huck Finn and Harry Potter, Pip and Pollyanna, Dorothy Gale and Daenerys Targaryen—those personalities remain with us. However, their escapades are purely imaginary, but our protagonist is the real deal.

Twenty minutes after they discovered her, she was having a big dinner and a warm bath, both of which she need. Then, for the first time in memory, she slept soundly. When she awoke, she was led to a classroom, where she joined a few other recruits at various stages of the Program.

Our protagonist was a natural. Her tutors referred to her as "focused" and "a quick study." Their attention was drawn to her demeanor rather than her aptitude. In every trial, she remained unflappable, seemingly resistant to the stress and tiredness that the Program was supposed to cause. Her professors were impressed. On Halloween, barely one week after discovering her alone and freezing on the city's rough streets, the decision was made.

They awoke her before morning and led her into a small room. It was inadequately insulated and rather cramped. She was sat on a drab leather cushion and told to be as still as possible.

Wires were dangling from devices and hooked to her skin.

Food and water were placed within easy reach.

Our protagonist remained calm. She asked no questions and only smiled as the men locked the door behind them.

Outside, the instructors gathered around a monitor to watch. Most recruits lasted around fifteen or twenty minutes before the claustrophobia became too much to endure. She was different. Unfazed, she lay there for an hour, then another, and another, gazing quietly at the gray metal ceiling a foot above her head and smiling the same odd smile.

The sound around her became more intense. So did her speed. Within minutes, she was hurtling through the troposphere, stratosphere, mesosphere, and thermosphere, entering space at 18,000 mph. She was an orphan, 4,000 miles above the streets she used to roam—the first of her species to orbit the Earth.

Those of you who remember the early days of the space race may recall how the world held its breath while hoping for her safe return.

Her name was Laika, and while she was undoubtedly feminine, she was not a woman. She was a trusting terrier with a questioning smile, a calm demeanor, and ears that bent in multiple directions at once. You see, the Soviets chose their first cosmonaut from the chilly streets of Moscow because they required a hardy specimen—a cadet who could withstand the cold of an inadequately insulated spacecraft. In other words, they wanted a dog with the correct qualities.

Today, Laika's sacrifice is well-known in Moscow.

Full disclosure: That last story almost broke me. It was the first one I wrote for The Way I Heard It, and it generated more sad-faced emojis and disappointed emails than any of the others. It also inspired an angry voice mail from my mother.

Interesting. I've written lots of stories about man's inhumanity to man, but that was the one story that upset my mother. My girlfriend, Sandy, didn't take it well, either. At the end of Laika's sad tale, she threw her headphones across the room.

"The Russians built her a statue?" she said. "Who cares? Those godless bastards sent her into space for seven days with just one meal? What a bunch of cold-blooded scumbags."

I don't have much sympathy for Michael Vick, either. Were those people simply overwhelmed by the sheer volume of human suffering in the world? It's easy, these days, to turn on CNN, pick up the paper, or scroll through your news feed and conclude that the world's gone to hell. Maybe it has. But is it really worse than it's ever been? I don't think so.

Is that why the story of one little dog—who died alone, with her little heart racing, way out in space—cut so deeply?

The truth is, I didn't sit down to write about Laika just because I disapproved of the way she was treated. Nor did I write about her to provoke my mother into a fit of profanity; that was just a bonus. I wrote about Laika because, once upon a time, she brought the whole world together. The one Sandy plucked from a pound in Marin and brought to our apartment in San Francisco.

It was an amazing thing to behold: my little mutt had the whole Internet by the tail.

After much consideration and some decidedly nonscientific methodologies, I selected the six most popular names. I unfolded a pee pad with six squares on it and wrote one name on each square. Then I set up a camera and waited for my puppy to poop, assuring my Facebook followers that I'd name him according to whatever name he pooped upon. Coincidentally (or maybe not?) the puppy pooped on "Freddy"—the name of my beloved high school teacher and mentor. What were the odds? One in six, I suppose. Looking back, though, it feels inevitable.

Chapter 12: SOMETHING IS MISSING

A young officer in a key battle, frustrated by his general's hesitation, takes matters into his own hands. He leaps onto his faithful steed and gallops to the front of the line to rally his warriors.

"He was suddenly in the front of the line," recalled one soldier, "his eyes flashing, pointing with his saber to the advancing foe, with a voice that rang clear as a trumpet."

"He came from nowhere," another claimed, "and electrified the soldiers. He merely wanted us to follow him, and so we did.

In a completely bold move, the young commander led three thousand soldiers directly into the flank of a superior foe, scattering the enemy and allowing his general to march his remaining army straight across the battlefield and win the day. But alas, something was missing. Specifically, the general's remaining troops.

Incredibly, the general had been concerned about the incorrect thing: who would receive credit for the win. So he withdrew his remaining forces and settled for a draw.

Three weeks later, when both sides clashed on the same bloody fields, it was deja vu all over again: at the critical moment, the general paused, and once again, the ambitious young officer jumped on his trusty steed and rode to the front lines—this time in direct defiance of his angry commander. When he neared the front line, he reared back on his horse. He cried to the troops again, "Hello, old buddies! So nice to see you again. What say you? Will we finally win the day? Should we send these thugs back across the sea?"

There are rare moments that turn the tide of every fight; rare battles that turn the tide of every war; and rare wars that change the course of human history. That was one of those moments in a combat during one of those conflicts. As at the Battle of Hastings in 1066, when William, Duke of Normandy, defeated England. As in the Battle of Orléans in 1429, Joan of Arc saved France. As with D-Day in 1944, when Dwight D. Eisenhower led the Allied invasion into Normandy. The heroes of the conflicts were honored for their courage. One became a king, another a saint, and one a president. All were recognized with statues that still stand today.

So, too, was the young officer with the broken leg who lay beneath his horse 240 years ago. Indeed, on that precise location today, you can still see the monument to our hero, raised a century after his triumphant charge and sculpted in granite to last through the centuries.

That is tremendous praise. If you visit this monument, you may notice that something is missing. For begin, consider the hero's eyes. His eyes are not triumphantly looking out over the Hudson Valley, as one might assume, because his statue lacks a head. His left hand does not hold the reins of his loyal steed, and his right hand does not point a gleaming saber at the enemy—because his statue lacks arms.

And then you'll understand why. The young officer who is commemorated in such an unusual manner forgot to do something on that dreadful day—he forgot to die. Pity.

Unfortunately, our hero not only survived the combat, but he also refused to have his crippled limb amputated. His ego wouldn't allow it. He spent the rest of his life in constant pain, hobbling around on a left leg three inches shorter than the right while completely ignoring the less obvious injury that would fester in ways that no doctor could treat: a wound to his pride, which eventually destroyed the only thing he valued more than his life.

Who knows. If General Gates had just acknowledged his young officer's extraordinary courage rather than taking all of the glory for himself, our hero could have taken different decisions following his injuries at Saratoga. Perhaps then he would have received a decent memorial.

Instead, he received The Boot, the only statue ever dedicated to a specific military hero that omits one unique detail: the hero's name.

In 2002, an artisan from Oakland offered to cast me in bronze for free. Though it was tempting to believe differently, his generous gift had nothing to do with me and was entirely focused on free exposure. As the host of a long-running, inexplicably popular TV show in San Francisco, I had grown accustomed to this type of quid pro quo.

As one of the hosts, my role was to introduce these squishy little parts from a different place each night—usually a five-star spa, a museum opening, or the newest Michelin-rated restaurant on Nob Hill. Not exactly meaningful job, but I was good at it and willing to accept the many benefits that came with being a local star.

My cameraman and I drove to an artist's studio in Oakland. I sat there for dozens of shots, each taken from a little different perspective, until every square centimeter of my massive cranium was documented. We created the initial mold and negative using those photographs and a mystery software tool. Several weeks later, we returned to film me pouring bronze into the negative. Then we returned to reveal the finished product.

Everyone won. Viewers received a fun glimpse at a fascinating procedure. The artist received a torrent of inquiries from other narcissists, all of whom were willing to spend $15,000 for a permanent reminder of their favorite subject. And I received my long-awaited trophy: a three-dimensional, two-hundred-pound selfie.

My joy was fleeting, however. Where precisely does one show a 200-pound replica of one's own head? In the entryway? On the piano? Atop the mantle? Sandy and I lived in a modest apartment, which seemed too small for this gigantic doppelgänger. "It's too heavy for the mantel," she explained. "And we don't own a piano. Or an entryway. Plus, I dislike how it looks at me." She said, sensing my disappointment, "Maybe I'll feel differently after you're dead?"

Think about this: It took us a century to give Benedict Arnold his memorial. That gave subsequent generations ample time to reflect on the depth of his treachery as well as his bravery on that particular ground. As a result, he received the memorial he deserved, which has yet to be toppled. But if Sandy's right, and animal lovers understand the Russians created

Chapter 13: WORDS, WORDS, WORDS

George understood the implications of words better than most. As did his son. But now, staring blankly at the tombstone that would be his son's last resting place, George couldn't find the appropriate ones. What words could possible sum up the poet's life, which was now being mourned by millions of people worldwide? "Loving son" ? That would not work. "Beloved husband and father" ? Hardly.

In the end, George chose "Kata ton daimona eaytoy." "True to his own spirit."

George was satisfied with these words. He hoped James would approve. However, George had never secured consent from James. To be fair, it was not something George had ever offered his rebellious kid. Indeed, father and son had not spoken since the tragic day James informed the elderly man that he was joining a band.

"A band?" "What kind of band?"

"A rock & roll band. "I am going to be the singer."

"That's ridiculous," George scoffed. "Rock & roll is not music. Besides, you can't even sing.

Now, looking down at the granite bust of the young guy with the long hair and the unearthly eyes, he reflected on the gravity of his wrong evaluation.

Back then, George was guarding a tense and dangerous coastline in an area that most Americans had never heard of. The seas were high that evening, the fog was thick, and the radar screen indicated hostile ships approaching from multiple directions—and swiftly.

Those statements reached the gunners, who, unlike George's son, were unlikely to defy his commands. For nearly four hours, George's navy fired on enemy ships that wouldn't leave his radar screen.

Meanwhile, thousands of miles away in Washington, DC, President Johnson learned of the maritime fight. He stopped all three networks with his own words: "This new act of aggression on the high seas must be met with a positive reply."

George informed his Hawaii-based commanders of the error. They quickly called McNamara, but for whatever reason, the secretary of defense failed to deliver the message to the president. The air attacks went off as planned, and we were immediately at war with Vietnam.

Yes, George realized the ramifications of his statements.

They had separated his family by speaking in fury. They had mistakenly divided his land.

It was Saturday morning. When I was fourteen, my father stood at the foot of my bed, honing a double-sided ax.

"It's time," he stated. "Let's go."

My father has a habit of starting discussions in the middle of sentences. He is also wary of anything modern, such as nouns.

"Time for what?"

I knew the question was futile before I asked it. So, as I slid out of bed and put on my pants and work boots, I tried again: "Is it cold out?"

"Invigorating," he said. "Your mom prepared oatmeal.

The man took considerable joy in locating the perfect tree. What he enjoyed even more was chopping down the tree.

Once that was done, we'd peel the limbs and branches and chop them into stove-length pieces. Then we'd focus on the trunk, working backward from the tree's top to its base. As the cuts grew thicker, the chainsaw wailed louder and higher.

"Sharpen the blade, son! "A dull one is twice as dangerous."

Even after the saw was turned off and stowed, I recall how my arms shook.

A wise guy named Einstein once stated, "People enjoy cutting wood. This practice produces immediate results."

Today, I wonder if the Morrisons had a woodpile behind their house. Where could George show Jim the consequences of cutting against the grain? A place to show the repercussions of driving wedges too deeply into the most obstinate stumps? From my experience, I know that fathers and sons can find the appropriate words. They can be seen in the woods when they go together to obtain the fuel they require to keep their family warm.

Chapter 14: CALL IT WHAT YOU WILL

Peter stood dumbfounded at the doorway of his bathroom, searching for the perfect word. "Ghastly" sprang to mind, followed in no particular sequence by "grisly," "gruesome," and "graphic." Sir Samuel Romilly, Peter's uncle, was sitting on the toilet floor, surrounded by his own blood. Moments before, the two men were in the study, discussing the "Treasure House" that Peter had been working on. Sir Samuel then got up from the couch, went into the bathroom, took up a straight razor, and drew the blade across his neck.

"Dear God," Peter exclaimed as he raced to Sir Samuel's side. "What have you done?"

The solution was obvious: Samuel Romilly had severed his carotid artery and windpipe. The poor man, heartbroken by the death of his beloved wife three days before, had fallen into a deep depression. Was there something more than grief? Despair, perhaps? Devastation? Despondency?

The mental torment had been too much for Sir Samuel to handle, and Peter could only watch as his uncle attempted to jot his final thoughts on a piece of bloodied stationery.

"My dear," he wrote. "I wish..."

He could not find the proper words. Instead, he sat there, bleeding on the bathroom floor and stared at the blank page. He died moments later, in his nephew's arms.

Peter was no longer dumbfounded. He had progressed to traumatized. Nonplussed. Astonished. Shocked, he did what he always did when the volatility of an unpredictable world threatened to overtake him. He returned to his study, opened the Treasure House, and began writing.

Two years later, sitting alone in the gloom of his parlor, Peter was looking for the perfect word. Was he depressed? Probably.

Call it whatever you want, but as Peter contemplated the precise nature of his malaise, ennui, languor, and lugubriousness, he couldn't help but observe that the wheels on the carriages passing by his window looked to be breaking the rules of physics. At least that's what they saw through the slats of his partially open shutters. Interesting.

Call it what you want, but Peter was obviously onto something. So, once again, he grabbed for his Treasure House, which was much thicker than it had been two years ago.

Now, I might simply say, "That's the way I heard it"—and divert your attention to Hollywood, where the name of the man most responsible for inventing the motion picture camera is recognized today with a star on the Hollywood Walk of Fame. I could, but I won't because, oddly, or perhaps paradoxically—or better still, unjustly—Peter's name is absent.

It's also not in the hallways of NASA, despite the fact that Peter devised the slide rule, a mathematical breakthrough that allowed us to land a man on the Moon.

The point is that we remember this prodigy, polymath, and pansophic for his great amount of words rather than his incredible list of accomplishments. Specifically, he compulsively collected a list of words to counteract the despair that affected him on a daily basis.

I'm referring, of course, to the indispensable directory of dialectical determination, which was designed to dramatically increase the word count of every term paper ever written, authored, or penned, while also assisting millions of aspiring writers in proving conclusively that "alliteration almost always annoys." I'm talking about an unrivaled linguistic lineup of syntactical substitutions; a critical compendium of etymological choices; a single source of all things synonymous, founded in serendipity and dedicated to the premise that no crossword puzzle should ever remain unfinished.

A amazing collection, which Peter Roget dubbed his "Treasure House." Alternatively, if you like Latin... his Thesaurus.

A time back, on a flight to Baltimore—the same aircraft I'm on right now—I came upon an Atlantic story about Roget. It was not complimentary.

The essay was written by Simon Winchester, who has worked on documentaries for the History and Discovery channels. I've had the pleasure of narrating several. Winchester also authored an excellent book, The Professor and the Madman, on the creation of the Oxford English Dictionary. I would recommend it. Actually, I just did. But I was astonished to learn that, to put it mildly—or politely or reticently—Winchester was not a fan of Roget's Thesaurus. According to Winchester, Roget discouraged rather than encouraged good writing. According to the Atlantic, "good writing" is less about finding the proper word and more about "the brave employment of the words that one already knows."

Chapter 15: THE BISCUIT BOMB

Rodman appeared constipated. The young private's attitude was one of constant concentration, broken occasionally by a crooked smile that came for no apparent reason.

In contrast, what about his best friend? Private Levy was the platoon's uncontested leader. He had proven himself to be an excellent storyteller both in the barracks and on the battlefield. In fact, you could argue that The Sopranos, Breaking Bad, and many other legendary TV shows would never have been if not for this nineteen-year-old private's incredible contribution during WWII.

But, of the numerous anecdotes Private Levy would tell, the most impactful occurred beneath a palm tree on the bloody beach of a little island that most Americans couldn't locate on a map.

Rodman was present on that day, December 18, 1944, along with the rest of the platoon, and they were all listening to Melvin Levy's every word. They'd lost half of their original complement, yet in the midst of the chaos and mayhem, there stood Private Levy, holding court under a palm tree in the tropical heat, weaving his spell and eliciting laughs in a place where laughing was no longer among the natural sounds.

Rodman stood off to the side, smiling crookedly, seeming strangely constipated, and admiring his friend's storytelling abilities.

A bombardier opened the doors of his DC-3 at that very time, high above them and possibly a quarter mile to the south. The boys dubbed those crates "biscuit bombs," and with no supply lines to rely on, they waited eagerly for those lifesavers to fall from the sky.

The 511th's troops were spellbound on the ground. Private Levy was approaching the conclusion of his story. All of his stories included unexpected turns, and the men had no idea where this one was going. For a few fleeting seconds, the fatigued warriors forgot about the threat that surrounding them, as well as their growing hunger. They were all lost in Private Levy's surprising story.

The biscuit bomb was traveling at around 200 miles per hour 20 feet above their heads. A half second later, it landed directly on Private Levy, and that was all. The soldier was crushed by the care box that was supposed to save his life.

That evening, Rodman—the platoon's only other Jewish child— wrote a eulogy for Private Levy. The following morning, he recited the eulogy to the rest of the platoon in a clear, well-modulated baritone. His comments, precisely metered and delivered with great care, expressed the underlying fear of living in a world beyond his comprehension—a world where assurance was not for sale. A world in which a massive box of biscuits could fall from the sky and pulverize your best friend.

The untimely death of Private Melvin Levy altered Rodman's life forever. He maintained his crooked smile, stilted voice, and vague expression of chronic constipation. However, the decision was made at that point. Private Levy's bizarre, horrible death had opened a portal through which Rodman eagerly stepped.

Chapter 16: THE MEN BEHIND BARS

Jimmy managed a very profitable business for a huge corporation in a very competitive industry. After only two years, his revenue was in the tens of millions of dollars, and his consumers were hopelessly addicted. The boss was satisfied. Extremely satisfied. But on February 12, 1985, Nicky died, and things became complex.

At the same time, halfway across the country, an Indiana farm child faced a completely other kind of difficulty. Tracy's father had been arrested for murder and condemned to life in prison. Clearly, the conviction was unjustified. The state had spent millions of dollars prosecuting Tracy's father, whilst the defense had spent less than $7,000 defending him. In addition, the clever guy who reportedly hired the boy's father to assassinate a judge was released as part of a plea bargain. To top it all off, the judge who sentenced Tracy's father to life in prison had been one of the victim's pallbearers!

The entire setting stunk. Tracy was determined to obtain his father an appeal. Of course, that would necessitate the hiring of a real lawyer, which would cost real money. So the twenty-four-year-old farm boy from Indiana did what he felt compelled to do: he took a new name and started seeking for the type of work that paid the amount of money he need.

Tracy had no expertise in this field, but he knew a few people who could help him make some introductions—and one of those individuals knew a man who connected him to another guy who set up a meeting with Jimmy.

It was a watershed event for the child from Indiana. When he strolled into Jimmy's pub for a seat, he couldn't help but feel nervous.

"You know who I am?"

Tracy nodded. "Yes, Sir. Your name is Jimmy, but I'm not sure if that's what I should call you. Sir."

Jimmy smiled. The child had an openness about him. His midwestern charm could be beneficial if he has additional attributes that compensated for Nicky's special talents.

Yes, it was a leap of faith. However, such decisions are often made. So Jimmy recruited a child from Indiana to replace Nicky's shoes, and to everyone's relief, Tracy fit right in. Not only did the labor come easy, but the pay exceeded his expectations. Much better. Before enough, he had enough money to employ the greatest attorneys in the country and put them to work evaluating the dubious case that had landed his father in a maximum security jail.

Tracy's father was, in fact, a hitman—a natural-born killer. Even while the circumstances preceding his final conviction were obviously shady, the overall picture of his life did not reflect that of a model citizen. This is why he was refused his appeal. That's why he died in prison, twenty-two years after his son walked inside one to interview for the position that altered his life.

"To live outside the law, you must be honest."

That's a direct quotation from Bob Dylan, and it occurred to me while I was sitting at the bar in Grumpy's writing the narrative you just read. Was Charles Harrelson an honest man? Was he honest with his fellow criminals? Was he honest with his son? With himself?

The bartender at Grumpy's had no answers but told me Bob Dylan was his favorite artist of all time. "An absolute genius," he said. Why don't you write a narrative about him? "Did you know he won the Nobel Prize?"

I swallowed some Anchor Steam and nodded. "I heard about that," I said. "Maybe I will."

I never wrote the story. But if I had, I would have titled it "The Big Lie"—because Bob Dylan was not a prisoner to the truth.

It is true. Bob Dylan lied his way through numerous news conferences. He stole tunes, arrangements, and lyrics from friends and predecessors alike.

Long before fake news became a serious issue for legitimate journalists, there was a real show about genuine news and false journalists: The Daily Show. On that broadcast, Jon Stewart mocked every aspect of news production.

But my friend Jon Stewart experienced an unusual phenomenon: the less genuine he looked to be, the more trusted he became. And the more trustworthy he got, the more seriously he was treated. It was intriguing to see, especially as individuals disagreed with him. "Hey, folks," he said. "What's the issue here?" "I'm just a guy making jokes." However, now that everyone trusted him, no one believed him. Poor Jon. He just couldn't have it both ways. Suddenly, millions of Americans were going to The Daily Show for legitimate news—Jon Stewart was "more trusted" than any actual anchorman—and Comedy Central was "more credible" than FOX and CNN. Is it any wonder that false news has become a reality?

Chapter 17: A MANLY MAN, A GOLD MEDAL, AND A REALLY BIG SEA

Long before he won the gold medal that now adorns his mantel, the Manly Man stood in the beach at the tip of Balboa Peninsula, smoking a cigarette and marveling at the largest waves he'd ever seen.

"God Almighty," he declared. "That is a really big sea."

The Olympic champion stood next to him, smiling and nodding. Monstrous breakers, driven to towering heights by an offshore gale, were forced together at the last minute by a chain of jetties guarding Newport Harbor. Local surfers dubbed it "the Wedge." Sensible people referred to it as a death trap.

Wally O'Connor called it a challenge.

"You're right," Wally replied. "This is a really large sea. Isn't this fantastic?"

The Manly Man felt adrenaline coursing through his body. This was how he felt every week on the football field, just before the bone-jarring hit at the line of scrimmage decided who stayed standing and who fell to the ground. He was addicted to the feeling, which is why he was drawn to Wally's risky new fad.

"I'll take the first pass," Wally announced. "Watch and learn."

The Manly Man returned to the crowd, smoked another Camel, and watched Wally O'Connor glide across the water. It was easy to understand why he had won gold in Paris.

Wally eased himself into the pipeline while extending one hand in a "stop" signal. His upturned palm sliced into the big rumbling wall of water, as his other arm stayed tucked behind him. Wally rocketed toward the coast like Superman, white foam exploding from his chest and green water smashing over his head. No one has ever seen anything like it: surfing without a board! As the mighty wave crashed in around him, Wally stroked hard, staying just ahead of the thunderous crash that sent him flying toward the beach like a human missile in a sea of foam, skimming across the surface before sliding gracefully onto the sand, where the locals greeted him with wild applause.

Wally rose up, gave a modest bow, and turned to the Manly Man, who had yet to win a gold medal.

"You're awake, champion. Ready?"

The large man nodded. "I am." A simple response to a simple question altered the path of his life.

The Manly Man faced the vast sea with manly confidence, emulating what he had seen Wally do. He swam against the rip tide for a hundred yards. He waited for a wave the size of Wally's. When it arrived, he jumped into its base, pushed off the shallow bottom, and emerged from the white water, where he began to soar, just like Wally.

But here's the thing: if you're going to compete with the vast sea, you'll need more than just male confidence; you'll also need impeccable timing. When the wall of water around him began to crumble, the Manly Man found himself in an awkward position. Thus, his manly body was propelled with enormous velocity not toward the shore, but directly toward the shallow bottom.

In the back of the ambulance, broken and fortunate to be alive, the Manly Man smoked another Camel. Did he anticipate that the only employment he'd be able to obtain during that year would be in the props department at 20th Century Fox? Did he anticipate that moving objects between sets would result in an audition and a name change to something more masculine? Probably not. But one thing is certain: the Manly Man could not have predicted the news conference he would hold in his home room thirty-five years later. The one performed only four days following his surgery.

In his Encino home, the Manly Man, now with his Manly Name but still without a gold medal, delivered an Oscar-worthy performance. He smiled proudly despite awful pain and spoke confidently to the Hollywood press, assuring them that he was ready to get back in the saddle. He did not show them the massive purple scar on his left side. He didn't talk about the lung that had just been removed or the four ribs he was now missing. He didn't mention the stitches that kept ripping open whenever he coughed, or the pail of phlegm and mucus upstairs by his bed. He didn't even mention the disease's name.

"I've licked 'the Big C' before," he informed journalists. "I will lick it again. Trust me, fellas, when I go out, it will be with both feet."

The reporters were thrilled. Nobody had ever called it "the Big C" before. Nobody had ever dismissed it as nothing more than a minor inconvenience. If anyone could overcome the disease, it would undoubtedly be the Manly Man, who had reduced it to a nickname. And, indeed, he did, completing two dozen feature pictures over the next twelve years, including the one that eventually earned him an Oscar.

But here's the thing: if you want to go head to head with the actual Big C, you'll need more than just male confidence. You will need to quit smoking. Unfortunately for the Manly Man, that was just too much to ask. So the man who had beaten the Japanese, the Mexicans, the Nazis, the Viet Cong, the Mongols, and too many Indians to count, in too many westerns to remember, was eventually defeated by a deadly horde of unfiltered Camels: five packs a day for four decades and more.

In the end, the man who shot Liberty Valance lacked the determination to quit smoking.

Today, his Manly Name is associated with a cancer organization, a park in Newport Beach, an airport in Orange County, and over 200 film credits. It's the same name that appears on the back of the gold medal he finally received, in the hospital, one month before his death, in 1979: a Congressional Gold Medal embossed with the name that we all know today, thanks to the Manly Man's run-in with the really big sea—a run-in that changed his life—and the really big C that ended it.

John Wayne, born Marion Morrison, had a successful career despite his unfortunate death.

Chapter 18: A TALE OF TWO PUPILS

George Underwood, fifteen years old, punched his attractive saxophone player. His motivation? An awful exhibition of skulduggery that could not be overlooked. A highly unforgivable betrayal, exacerbated by the fact that the attractive saxophone player in question was George Underwood's closest friend.

Here's what occurred: In the spring of 1962, George and his best friend were students at Bromley Technical High School for Boys. They were members of George and the Dragons, a band you've probably never heard of. He definitely had the looks for it. George was also incredibly attractive and charismatic. His presence jumped off the stage, he had a powerful voice, and his Elvis impersonation always made the young girls swoon.

Anyway, George had planned a date with Carol Goldsmith, the attractive schoolgirl he'd been eyeing all semester. But a few hours before their scheduled meeting at the youth center, George's saxophone player took him aside.

"Hi, George. I recently saw Carol at the record store. She stated she couldn't make it this evening. Between you and me, I believe she is seeing someone else.

George was understandably sad, but he appreciated the heads-up from his faithful bandmate.

The next day at school, George discovered the betrayal and reacted as any young man brimming with testosterone and righteous wrath would. He approached his treacherous bandmate, confirmed his deception, and landed a roundhouse hit that left his best friend flat on his back with a black eye and a swollen face.

Actually, the consequences were worse than that. George Underwood's rage earned him the disdain of everyone at Bromley Tech, including his teachers, his best friend's parents, and Carol Goldsmith.

But all of that would happen later. On that particular day in 1962, George's saxophone player was transported to the hospital, where he spent many weeks while physicians attempted to repair the harm George had caused. Fortunately, they didn't succeed. The official diagnosis was "anisocoria," and after two procedures, doctors declared the damage irreversible.

George would carry the shame for the rest of his life. But he wouldn't go unforgiven. In reality, a few months later, George and his saxophone player joined the Konrads, a band you've probably never heard of. Following the Konrads, they founded the Hooker Brothers, which you've most likely never heard of, and then the King Bees, which may also be unfamiliar. Along the way, however, George realized that regardless of what they called themselves, people came to watch his disfigured but still gorgeous saxophone player, not to hear him sing. He irreparably altered the visage of his best friend.

Chapter 19: THE 25-MILLION-DOLLAR KISS

Hedwig was stunning and married to a guy she did not love. Fritz was an arms merchant who was extremely attached to his trophy bride.

Hedwig disliked fascists and Nazis. She didn't want them in her house or on her table, and she despised the fact that her husband was selling them guns. As yet another dinner party neared, Hedwig chose the most glamorous evening gown from her extensive wardrobe.

In fact, Hedwig was so lovely that she was thought "too beautiful to speak"—and hence received very little words on TV. When asked to describe the secret of being glamorous, Hedwig said, "That's easy. "All you have to do is stand there and look stupid."

But Hedwig was not foolish. Far from it.

Hedwig had heard that the Allies couldn't sink German U-boats because the Germans had figured out how to jam the torpedoes' radio channels. She remembered a scientist from one of those dinner gatherings in Vienna. He had been discussing with Fritz the untapped potential of radio waves in modern warfare.

Hedwig pondered, "What if a single radio transmission could jump arbitrarily from one frequency to another? "How would the Nazis stop that?"

The question was clever, as was the solution.

She created the technology, patented it, and gave it to the navy free of charge. The navy was not interested in her suggestion. In reality, Hedwig was informed that if she truly wanted to support the war effort, she needed to employ the attributes for which she was most famous.

Hedwig was upset, but she knew she had the assets in question and was anxious to contribute—in any way she could—to winning the war. So, to raise funds for war bonds, she started selling kisses. In one night, she raised $7 million simply by "standing still and looking stupid." She ultimately raised $25 million. In today's dollars, that is more than $220 million.

Even if the story had ended here, it would have been an excellent headline: "The most beautiful girl in the world fights Nazis with kisses!" But Hedwig's story was far from finished. During the Cuban Missile Crisis in 1962, her technology was finally put to use—and it worked. Big-time.

Hedwig received no appreciation or gratitude. She did not ask for any. But let's be completely clear about the immensity of the notion she had patented. Not only did "radio hopping" change the face of national security, but it also paved the way for the development of our modern-day satellite communications infrastructure and the useful technology known as "Wi-Fi." Without her innovation, I would never have been able to explore her life at 37,000 feet and share it with you—the narrative of a beautiful girl who realized which assets were most important. Hedy Lamarr was a movie star.

That struck me as a story worth sharing for a variety of reasons, the most important of which is that I would not have been able to write these stories without her creation.

Chapter 20: THE MYSTERY OF THE VANISHING WOMAN

The woman booked into the resort on her own. She arrived without reservation or luggage. She signed the guest book as Miss Neele and stated that she was visiting from Cape Town, South Africa, which is 8,500 kilometers south.

Miss Neele kept a low profile during the next twenty-four hours. A sharp-eyed banjo player recognized her from a photo in the newspaper. The banjo player was aware that there was a reward for her concern. He immediately alerted the authorities. Moments afterward, detectives were on their way from London, believing Miss Neele might help solve a missing persons case unlike any other.

The investigation began two weeks earlier, when a car was discovered on a steep hill near the Silent Pool, a disused rock quarry. The car's windshield was cracked. The headlights were still on. Inside, the police discovered a luggage, a fur coat, and a driver's license belonging to one of England's most well-known women. Detectives had suspected a kidnapping based on the woman's riches, but there was no ransom message. They interviewed scores of people, including the woman's husband. He feared that his wife had committed suicide.

"She's been in a terrible state," Archie added. "She has been profoundly depressed ever since her mother died. It's been fairly bad."

Police threw pronged hooks on ropes into the Silent Pool and dragged a body. Bloodhounds were dispatched. Fifteen thousand volunteers combed the landscape from Guildford to London. For the first time, airplanes were used to hunt for a missing individual. Arthur Conan Doyle, the author of Sherlock Holmes, paid for the services of a medium. Unfortunately, no luck.

The mystery captivated the British press.

"A Suicide with No Corpse!" the headlines said.

"A Murder with No Suspects!"

"A Kidnapping with No Ransom!"

Across the ocean in New York, the Times covered the mystery on its front page with a simple headline: "Who Done It?" But "Who done it?" wasn't really the question. The actual inquiry was, "What happened?"

How could a woman so famous simply vanish off the face of the Earth?

Then Scotland Yard began to investigate the matter. Detectives discovered that Archie had requested a divorce a month earlier, but his vanished wife had refused. Interesting. They also discovered that Archie stood to inherit a large sum of money if his wife never returned. That was also intriguing. It provided them with a motive, but Archie had an alibi. On the night his wife vanished, he was at a dinner party with numerous others, all of whom confirmed his presence. Then there was another development in the case: one of the witnesses turned out to be Archie's young secretary—a young secretary who, it turned out, was having an affair with him. A young secretary named Miss Neele.

Archie acknowledged to the affair right away, but even after being questioned for several hours, he swore that he had no information of his missing wife's location. At this point, the detectives focused their attention on Miss Neele. What did the young secretary tell the cops about the inexplicable disappearance of the woman whose husband she adored? Clearly, this woman needed to be probed. So she was.

Detectives gathered on the peaceful resort in North Yorkshire. Inside, the band played while visitors danced and dined. The banjo player noticed them and motioned toward the dining area, where they discovered "Miss Neele," who was playing bridge with a few other guests. Only the Miss Neele they discovered wasn't Archie's mistress. She was not Archie's secretary. She was not from South Africa. Miss Neele had no ID, no knowledge of how she had arrived at the hotel, and no idea why she had introduced herself as Miss Neele. Despite the fact that Miss Neele had no idea who she was, the detectives were certain. She was the woman who appeared on the top pages of every British newspaper. She was the elusive target of the biggest manhunt in English history. She had eventually been discovered, safe and sound and happy as a lark, 240 miles from her home, at a hotel where she had checked in under the name of her husband's lover. But why? Thus started the true mystery of the Vanishing Woman.

"For twenty-four hours," the lady replied, "I wandered in a dream, and then found myself in Harrogate as a well-contented and perfectly happy woman who believed she had just come from South Africa."

Doctors stated she had entered a "fugue state" caused by stress. They stated that in such a situation, a person could black out while staying completely cognizant. But when the story broke, it raised more questions than answers: how could the woman have gone unnoticed for so long when the entire country was seeking for her? She must have been aware of Archie's involvement with the genuine Miss Neele. Was her disappearance intended to disgrace her philandering husband? Had the spouse drugged her, possibly to render her insane and steal all of her money? Or was it all a marketing trick to promote her latest book?

Everyone had a theory, but no one had an idea.

Archie's soon-to-be ex-wife rapidly regained consciousness after being sent home. She divorced her husband, who soon married his secretary, the genuine Miss Neele. Then she left her home once more.

But here's an unusual thing: of all the mysteries surrounding this exceptional woman, the true story of her mysterious disappearance is mostly forgotten. It could be because, after returning from her trip to Baghdad, she declined to discuss the topic further. Even her autobiography does not mention the occurrence.

Twenty-one mysteries of Georgia Farm revealed themselves to me all at once in 1991, while I was snowed in and fighting to stay sane. I discovered them in Morris Stroud's study: a stack of dog-eared paperbacks by John D. MacDonald.

Chapter 21: HIS LAST LETTER HOME

The postman removed the rubber bands off the envelopes before sliding another stack of mail through the front door slot. Ingrid could hear the screech of the small hinge, the chirp of tin against tin, and the quiet whoosh of a new stack of mail landing on an old stack of mail. Those were the sounds she tried to ignore, the ones that signaled a fresh day of grief.

"I'm hungry, Mommy!" "I am hungry now!"

That was one sound she couldn't ignore.

In the kitchen, Ingrid smeared peanut butter on toast for her two-year-old son while the phone jangled in its cradle. "Hello," she whispered. "Yes, this is she. Yes, he would have turned 31 in January. "You are welcome."

Ingrid left A.J. to his peanut butter toast and returned to the front door. With a bare toe, she moved away the catalogs and invoices to look at the dozens of sympathy cards—a literal pile of sadness she couldn't bring herself to read. But there, buried among the sympathies, Ingrid noticed the telltale handwriting. His penmanship. And a postmark dated September 23, 1973. She received a letter from her husband. A letter from beyond the dead.

Fort Jackson, SC. September, 1966. Ingrid's husband is simply another person waiting in line to make a phone call home. This private failed basic training due to what the army described as "issues with authority," which means he would be separated from his new bride for an additional six weeks. Ingrid will not be pleased.

As he waits his turn to give the bad news, the young soldier does what he always does: he observes others around him and fabricates stories to pass the time.

The truth was, Ingrid enjoyed all of his stories. But she never anticipated they'd make her rich or widowed. Nonetheless, six years had passed, and now she was here, her grief temporarily alleviated by the shock of receiving a telegram from the husband she had buried five days before. Moments later, overcome with grief, Ingrid attempted to make a long-distance call to her mother. However, when the operator heard Ingrid's last name, she hesitated.

Back in line, Ingrid's husband focuses his attention on the soldier in front of him. Red-rimmed eyes. The hunched shoulders. The balled-up fist was gently tapping on his new crew cut. He's definitely on the wrong end of a Dear John call. Ingrid's husband imagines the girl at the other end. A dishonest girl. A girl cheated on the soldier with his best friend.

The call terminates. The phone slips from the soldier's grasp and dangles in midair. Ingrid's husband is close enough to hear the operator remark, "Oh, honey, I'm very sorry. Are you still there? Would you like to make another call?

The soldier, blinking back tears, clutches the receiver and pours his heart out to the operator. Ingrid's spouse does not eavesdrop. He simply watches the soldier's expression and makes up a small fiction to pass the time.

Ingrid's spouse eventually leaves the army and returns home. Briefly. He continues to write stories, but when A.J. arrives and money becomes an issue, the former private begins presenting his tales to anyone willing to pay to hear them. Turns out, Ingrid isn't the only one who enjoys them. People think they feel really real. They claim his characters remind them of their own neighbors.

So the former private takes his stories on the road, and before long, the money starts rolling in. But being separated from his family is terrible. Ingrid misses her husband, A.J. misses his father, and the man who used to compose stories just to pass the time begins to fret over the days he will never have back. After an all-too-brief visit home, he writes a novel about a lonely troubadour who wishes to relive his best days over and over again. People enjoy that one, too. A lot.

Then, just as his career is taking off, Ingrid's spouse makes the unimaginable decision: he quits. In his final letter home, the young writer promises to begin creating all types of stories. Novels and screenplays. Anything that does not need to be repeated night after night. He concludes his letter with the following: "Remember, sweetheart, it's the first sixty years that count, and I have thirty more to go. "I love you."

Later that day, he mails the letter and takes a private plane, which crashes just after leaving the runway. Five days later, the postman on Ingrid's porch brings the best possible news at the worst possible moment.

Chapter 22: ONE HELL OF A TOLL

On the day of the grand celebration, the invalid peered through his telescope at the crowd assembled below. Thousands of people had already gathered. Hundreds more were on their way, hoping to watch the passenger embark on an extremely unusual journey—one that experts believed would never be finished.

The invalid pulled his chair up to the window and assessed the cost of the small journey. 15 million dollars. Twice as much as he had budgeted. The cost had gone out of hand. Way out of control. Unforgivably, absolutely out of control. Today, such extravagant spending is referred to as "business as usual." Back then, it was referred to as "the price of progress." In any case, $15 million for a ten-minute ride was an exorbitant price.

Through his telescope, the invalid observed the passenger approach the vehicle, turn to the collected crowd, and begin to talk. He couldn't hear the words but understood what was being conveyed. The traveler thanked the taxpayers for their patience. Thanking them for believing in the mission. Thanking them for the privilege of becoming the first to go where no man has gone before.

When the passenger concluded, the audience clapped enthusiastically. Fireworks erupted. The band started to play. Then, after fourteen years of meticulous planning, heartbreaking setbacks, and too many barriers to count, the passenger hopped into the vehicle, waved to the crowd, and drove off into history.

The patient, grimacing in misery with each breath, viewed everything through the lens of his telescope—and wept. Perhaps if his wife had been with him on that historic day, she could have alleviated his suffering. She'd been attempting to heal the unexplained ailments that had plagued him since his escape from that horrific fire sixty feet under the surface. They had started with unusual tingling in his feet and hands, then tremendous agony in his knees and elbows, and finally inexplicable bruises on his chest and ribs. The headaches had begun. He had headaches that made him wish he'd stayed below with the others who died in that pressured pit of despair. However, his wife had never left his side. Even when the swelling had rendered him speechless. Even when the numbness rendered him immobilized. Even as his skin began to molt and flake off in bits.

Today, we call it the bends. Back then, it was known as caisson sickness. In any case, the cost was exorbitant.

The invalid never recovered, but he stayed on the job, overseeing the development from his bedroom window, always behind his telescope and writhing with pain. His wife served as his nurse, ears, hands, and mouth, delivering his commands to the men laboring below. In her leisure time, she pursued physics, hydrodynamics, and structural engineering. When her husband's condition worsened, she started attending meetings that he couldn't. Meetings with corrupt politicians, vicious financiers, and a slew of unethical suppliers. Women were not welcome at these meetings. She went to them nonetheless. She lobbied hard to prove the experts wrong. In the end, she did.

The invalid watched the celebration unfold below him through his telescope, pondering the cost of advancement. Slowly, reluctantly, he turned his sight away from the triumphant passenger and back to the accident site. Not the accident that had rendered him disabled and devastated, but the one that had placed him in command. He pinpointed the exact location on the pier, half a mile distant. A slip, a tumble, a fractured foot, an amputation, an infection, and his father— the main engineer who had originally thought of this adventurous journey—was gone.

Of course, it didn't seem "just like that" at the time. The old man died after several weeks. He'd had unexplained spasms that stretched his spine backward, leaving his body arched and twisted. Then he'd dealt with spasms that forced his arms to twitch violently—before they, too, went rigid. He would never forget how his father's face had gradually receded from his head. The muscles in his head had tightened and seized, forcing his face backward. When his father eventually died, his eyes were big and bulging, and his teeth were bared in a dreadful grimace.

Today, we name it tetanus. They used to call it lockjaw.

In any case, the cost was exorbitant.

Chapter 23: BREAKING THE SILENCE

When Donald Crouch first met Jim in his English class in rural Michigan, he regarded him as a morose fourteen-year-old. A boy who had withdrawn deeply into a cocoon of self-imposed silence.

Donald may have assumed that Jim was bored, uninterested, or even backward. He certainly appeared to be all of these things. But there was something about the young boy that lit up whenever the topic turned to poetry. Donald saw a subtle alteration in the boy's posture—a modest but undeniable enthusiasm that accompanied any talk of Chaucer, Shakespeare, or Tennyson.

Donald once kept Jim after school and attempted to communicate with the stony-faced child. He quickly saw what the problem was: Jim stuttered. Not a little, but a lot.

The next day, Donald assigned his English students to create a poem. The topic did not matter as long as it was something the students felt passionate about. That's where fate intervened, as it frequently does—this time in the form of a ruby red grapefruit.

During the Great Depression, rickets and scurvy were a public health concern in Michigan. To remedy the situation, the government sent lots of fruit up from Florida.

Jim submitted his poetry the next day, and Donald was astounded by how brilliant it was. Then he did something most professors would never do nowadays: he put Jim on the spot. Donald had seen before that Jim's stutter disappeared when he quoted his favorite poets aloud. So, as he returned the students' assignments, complete with grades and comments, Donald addressed the class.

Jim froze in his seat. The blood surged to his face. He could feel the other students staring at him. Why would his teacher urge him to do this? Jim had placed his trust in Mr. Crouch. Now he felt betrayed. Donald's following words left Jim feeling doubly betrayed: "Jim, I believe your poem is too good to be true. Frankly, I don't believe you wrote it."

Jim may have been silent, but he had exceptional hearing. He could not believe his ears. Was Mr. Crouch accusing him of plagiarism?

As Robert Frost said, "way leads on to way," and Jim's path was immediately obvious. He became a master of memorizing. Reciting poems led to the formation of a debate group. The debate club led to the theater.

Following that, she received a Tony Award. Then an Emmy. Then, an honorary Oscar. The world seemed too little to contain a voice as powerful as Jim's, so he took on the cosmos. A galaxy far away...

That's how Darth Vader's villainous voice was born—coaxed from the body of a phenomenal performer who might have remained a more silent observer if not for an extraordinary teacher who understood the power of the spoken word and the unexpected arrival of a ruby red grapefruit that tasted too good to be true. The distinctive voice of... James Earl Jones.

Like James Earl Jones, I was a very timid child with a deep voice and a strange stammer. My mother still enjoys telling stories about how, as a boy, I'd dive beneath the dining room table when the doorbell rang. According to her, I used to puke just thinking about meeting new people.

When we first met, I was a tall, skinny freshman with an advancing hairline and a fist-sized larynx.

Remember George C. Scott's opening speech to Patton? Patton was a wimp compared to Fred King. He strolled into our classroom the first day and greeted us with two words that blended together: "Shutup!"

His voice was quite loud. The classroom became instantly quiet. In the quiet, he handed out a sheet of music that no one could sight-read. It was a six-part a cappella arrangement in Latin.

We had no way of orienting ourselves because we didn't know how to sight-read, and there was also no time. Mr. King had already blown the pitch pipe, raised his hands, and begun to conduct.

I'm not sure what he expected, but the silence that followed seemed to confuse him.

Mr. King looked around curiously. He stared down at his hands, as if they were causing the trouble. Then he frowned, repeated the pitch, and began directing again.

Silence.

"This is the Overlea High School Concert Choir, is it not?"

Again, quiet.

Mr. King closed his eyes. He took several long breaths, as if to relax himself. Then he became insane. Smashing one hand on the piano, he started into a diatribe laced with terms commonly heard in pool halls and saloons. He began to foam. He rants. He cursed like the sailor he once was as his neck and forehead veins bulged. He ripped the sheet music to tears, hurled the pieces into the air, and began ranting about "cruel twists of fate," "clueless mutes," and other topics.

Technically, we saw a "smile." I'd characterize it as a gash—a painful breach between the nose and the chin that reveals a rictus of rotting enamel. Tiny teeth—baby teeth—were jammed up against massive incisors. Molars erupted from areas generally allocated for canines. His front teeth, while well aligned, were the size of little fingers. They protruded past his ever-widening lips, as if attempting to escape the infected gums from which they hung.

Beth Johnson let out a gasp. Cindy Stone shouted.

"Ladies and gentlemen," he announced, "the cowards have all left. Let us have some fun.

For the following three years, we did. We talked. We laughed. We learned. We discovered that our teacher's genuine teeth had been knocked out on the gridiron years before, yet we continued to wonder. You never knew what Mr. King had in his mouth. You never knew what would come of it.

Mr. King went about his job of urging, exhorting, and encouraging his students without concern for the regular curriculum or political correctness. "Instructing" is an understatement: He pushed us harder than any other teacher had. He'd give us Vaughan Williams' Hodie and Bach's Mass in B Minor to sing—works so far beyond our abilities that we didn't know what to do.

It was an invaluable lesson. A lesson I would forget several times— in fact, you just witnessed me forget it a few paragraphs earlier, up on the Mackinac Bridge—but a crucial one nonetheless.

Anyway, as I was saying, I admitted to Mr. King early on that "I've never sung before."

In response, he assigned me a solo that was many notes beyond my range. He kept me after class for private voice lessons, and when he noticed I stuttered, he suggested I audition for the school play. By "suggested," I mean he demanded—and the outcome was devastating. Mr. King interrupted me while I was stammering my way through a monologue memorized the night before.

I did not think or resist. I did not argue. I just started again, and this time I did not stutter.

A light bulb came on. New possibilities arose before me. I began to act like someone who did not stutter. A more confident individual. For the time being, I'd settle for the lead role in one of our school plays and a new position in Fred King's great Chorus of the Chesapeake. From there, I'd play things as they were and try to remember the value of "what, not how."

A seemingly straightforward task that proved to be far more difficult than anticipated.

Chapter 24: THE BIGGEST NAME IN TOWN

On a bright September evening, a tenacious sun slowly sank in the hills of a heartless town, even as a young starlet strolled up the shoulder of some canyon road and out onto the property of the town's biggest name. She was naturally nervous. It was dark, she was trespassing, and she was going to commit a murder.

For the record, the superstar was not inherently violent. But dire times require desperate means. The studio's head, a huge figure in town, was also a feckless fool who lacked taste and common sense. He had almost completely cut her out of the film that would have made her famous.

Could she have phoned HR? Could she have made an official complaint to the studio? No. This treachery could not be fixed by a hashtag and a me-too. This was personal.

The iconic figure, five stories above her, peered down as the starlet approached. Her appearance was not particularly surprising. Beautiful girls often come to this location. Usually they arrived around sunset. This female, however, was rather attractive. She was twenty-four, with flaxen hair, alabaster skin, and eyes as blue as the Montana sky. Oh, yeah, girls like her were always welcome here. Pretty young things with stars in their eyes, eager to trade everything they had for the one thing they lacked.

Five stories below, the starlet smiled—despite her sinister mission. It felt great to fight back. She recounted the role that launched her career: a little but important role in a Broadway production of Hamlet. The starlet remembered that performance vividly. She felt confident that it was well worth an encore.

But enough about memories; let us return to the business at hand. She knew the way inside. She knew her target was on the top floor. In her mind's eye, she imagined herself gently ascending each step, one by one. The view from the summit was undoubtedly breathtaking.

The celebrity checked her handbag one last time. She ensured that everything was exactly where it should be. Then she began her careful trek up to the fifth floor, where she delivered an Oscar-worthy performance.

A hiker discovered the corpse three days later. A mangled body was found in a nearby ravine.

Detectives were called in, but it didn't take a hard-boiled gumshoe or a Sunset Boulevard shamus to find out who did it. The cops were well aware of the starlet's unexpected departure from Thirteen Women, her first and last major film. They were aware of the financial hardships that followed, as well as the nude images for which she had been paid to pose. But it was the contents of her handbag that sealed the case just moments after it had been opened—specifically, a brief letter that said, "I am afraid I am a coward. I apologize for everything. If I had done this sooner, I could have avoided a lot of pain."

And so ended Peg Entwistle's final act, a talented actress who quit a bright theater career to try her luck in Los Angeles.

It was the most well-known name in town.

Chapter 25: THE GREASEMAN COMETH

The grease worker dragged his shovel across the wooden floor and jabbed it into the towering pile of coal, sounding a pleasant crunch.

Technically, this was the fireman's job, but the grease worker wasn't complaining. In 1869, protesting about the Michigan Central Railroad got you nowhere. Lifting with his knees and twisting with his hips, the grease man swung his wrist, launching the anthracite into the air and seeing it disappear into the furnace's wide maw. The sounds of his job matched the speed of the train under him—a constant Sisyphean cadence driving man and machine into America's heartland.

Back then, locomotives were frequently shut down for oiling and loosening. Engines, wheels, and equipment were also produced at factories around the world. Everything that moved required lubrication, but nothing could be greased while moving. Thus, civilization's wheels could only turn as fast as the grease man worked. So, after ten minutes of contortions beneath numerous boxcars and within the engine, our hero emerged resembling a glazed doughnut. Sweat ran over his forehead, stinging his eyes. Chunks of animal fat adhered to his overalls and skin. Was he resentful? Did he imagine that his fancy apprenticeship at a prominent machine shop in Scotland qualified him for more than a job shoveling coal and slathering oil into the entrails of this iron horse? The quick response is, "No." But the grease man didn't think about it. He was too thirsty to think—extremely thirsty.

The grease worker refilled his empty cup and mused aloud, "What if a train could be hydrated just as easily as a human?"

It was a good question, and he spent the following year tinkering in his workshop, hoping to find an answer. Eventually, he perfected a prototype and filed for patent. His invention was straightforward: a reservoir of oil that used gravity to provide just enough lubrication to where it was needed while the engine was still operating. He named it a lubricant cup. If it succeeded, locomotive engines wouldn't have to stop to be greased. True, a mechanical solution would abolish his own position. Overall, it appeared to be a gamble worth taking.

As it turned out, the lubricating cup worked—and the effect on productivity and mobility was astonishing. Word of this discovery traveled throughout the country, and soon every engineer and conductor from Tacoma to Tallahassee was requesting one.

Obviously, the grease man wasn't in a position to go into large manufacturing. So, over the next few years, cheap imitations appeared everywhere. They all promised similar outcomes, but none were as dependable as the original.

Over the next sixty years, the grease man applied for and received fifty-six more mechanical patents. His work transformed the Industrial Revolution.

Thomas Edison said, "Genius is one percent inspiration and ninety-nine percent perspiration." If he had spoken with the grease worker, Elijah, he might have allocated a few percentage points to lubrication—and emancipation as well.

Elijah had an opportunity thanks to the Underground Railroad. Elijah's parents provided him with an apprenticeship. And, because to his hard ethic and insatiable desire to construct a better mousetrap, Elijah was able to achieve such success that his surname is still used today. You already know it. You've probably used it. The slave name has become linked with authenticity and originality, prompting the question, "Is that the real McCoy?".

"You can't script the Bering Sea."

Phil Harris said this during another After the Catch roundtable discussion. We were enjoying a round of duck farts and talking about the peculiar appeal of Deadliest Catch when Phil came up with the amazing response. He repeated it under his breath seconds later, as he lit another cigarette.

"You can't script the Bering Sea."

"Damn," I replied. "Why do you say the best stuff when the cameras aren't rolling?"

Phil shrugged. "Why do you ask the best questions during commercials?"

I laughed and asked the same question a few minutes later. But, of course, with the cameras running, Phil responded differently—as I expected him would.

"It's the narrator," he explained. "He's the key to our success." "That sexy devil could make anything seem exciting."

"Well," I replied, "there's no accounting for taste."

The captains chuckled, and we went on to another issue, but Phil's persistent refusal to repeat himself hit me yet again. He regarded second takes as a performance. It drove the producers crazy because Phil said so many wonderful things off camera. However, Phil believed that reality television should be authentic, and he worked hard to keep it that way

"What the hell happened?" he inquired at the following break. "One minute, I am watching Jacques Cousteau, Jane Goodall, and David Attenborough. Now all I see are'real' housewives who aren't genuine, and'survival' experts drinking their own pee. "What the hell is next?"

He threw another duck fart back and started another cigarette.

"You're right," I replied. Because he was. Not long after that chat, the Amish got a Mafia, the Ducks got a Dynasty, Honey got a Boo-Boo, and "reality" TV became deeply absurd. Today, it's about manufacturing moonshine, flipping houses, mining for gold, pawning junk in storage lockers, and getting shouted at by angry cooks who are paid to be upset. Everyone else is naked and afraid.

I've seen the scripts for some of those "unscripted" shows. Believe me, they exist, and they are as thorough as a sitcom or movie script. But one thing is certain: no matter how hard Hollywood works to "produce" reality, Phil got it right. You cannot script the Bering Sea.

Imagine Bourdain is twenty feet down with his cameraman and spear when store-bought frozen octopi float by his head. That's what any "reality" producer in my industry would do to "salvage" a scene—but it drives Bourdain insane. Later, in voice-over, he chastises the producer for attempting to deceive his audience and insists that CNN release the unedited tape. Which, to its credit, CNN does. When I met Tony, I complemented him on the episode. Tony, like Joan Rivers, Phil Harris, and the Bering Sea, cannot be scripted.

On the first season of Deadliest Catch, before anyone knew what the show would become, someone at the network believed crab fishing would make an excellent game show. I'm not kidding: as the emcee of whatever this thing was, I was told to award a cash reward of $250,000 to the "winning" boat live on camera. The brilliant producer who came up with the idea wasn't in Dutch Harbor when the Coast Guard commander learned about it, but I was.

"Are you people out of your minds?"

It was a generic inquiry directed at a small group of producers, cameramen, and myself.

"Gentlemen, this is the most perilous job on earth. "How much deadlier do you want it to be?"

The commander was looking right at me. It seemed disrespectful not to respond during the subsequent silence.

"Well, sir, I can't speak for the network, but it seems to me—"

"What's your name, son?"

The captain was my age yet addressed me as "son." How cool is that?

"I'm Mike Rowe," I introduced myself.

"Are you the star of the show?"

"No, I'm the host."

"Do you work for the Discovery Channel?"

"Yes, sir, I do."

"Then why the hell can't you speak for them?"

I understand the commander's frustration. Every week, the Coast Guard responds to several distress calls from fishing boats captained by mortal men who occasionally go too far in their rush to grab as much crab on board as possible. In the commander's perspective, we were idiots who had flown in from Hollywood to splash gasoline on an already out-of-control inferno.

The commander was not completely wrong.

"Trust me," I said. "I'm sure that my masters won't want to turn your crab season into a free-for-all."

The commander exhaled and shook his head. "You don't get it, son. It is already a free-for-all. And you're making things worse."

Once again, he was right to be concerned: viewing something always modifies its behavior. It's known as the "observer effect." It holds true in both physics and crab fishing. A Dutch film crew was determined to change things, whether or not they had $250,000. But the commander was not fully correct, either.

Two weeks after this chat, the Big Valley collapsed. However, there was no film crew on board. Nobody was there to watch it sink. Furthermore, injuries and fatalities did not increase once filming began. In fact, shortly after our first season aired, a new regulation was introduced that repealed the derby system, which many argued made crab fishing more dangerous than it needed to be. I could argue that our show made things safer. But I won't, since people still die up there, no matter how careful they are.

You cannot script the Bering Sea.

To make duck farts, mix Kahlúa, Bailey's, and whiskey. Layered in equal amounts in that specific order. They were Phil's favorite, but as I've often told him, there is no accounting for taste.

Chapter 26: A LITTLE TOWN UP NORTH

During her farewell tour in 2005, Cher insisted on having many boxes of aloe vera tissues in rose-scented, cube-shaped boxes in her dressing room at each stop.

Fortunately, Cher was not David's concern.

When Mariah Carey was interviewed on British television in 2009, she insisted that two stagehands lower her onto the sofa so that her dress would not crease.

Fortunately, Mariah was not David's concern.

When Madonna checked into a 5,000-square-foot hotel suite in 2012, she requested hundreds of pink flowers, individually arranged in hundreds of crystal vases and carefully placed on every flat surface.

Fortunately, Madonna wasn't David's problem either.

Eddie's requirement for seven weeks of preparation was David's dilemma. Because if David was going to pull off an event of this scale—the most ambitious outdoor gathering in recent memory—he'd need the perfect entertainment. Eddie was truly unique. But, seven weeks of rehearsal? That was a diva maneuver unlike anything David had ever witnessed. The event was less than a month away. Moving the date now would be a logistical headache. What to do?

David rubbed his painful temples and felt sorry for himself. Prima donnas were just as common in the 1960s as they are now, and boys like David were still at their mercy. However, David was also motivated by the 1960s to see this through. America was at war, young people were rebellious, and David believed the country could benefit from a widespread display of love and unity. He also thought that the farmland near his hometown would be an ideal location.

Of course, he was correct.

You're familiar with the town. You might even recognize the iconic address.

Again, you had to be present. But even if you weren't, Eddie was undeniably powerful. He could play for hours on end, as Hendrix and Joplin did. He, like the Grateful Dead and Jefferson Airplane, could riff in ways that wowed audiences and left them wanting more. However, unlike those legendary headliners, Eddie did not have a band to back him up. Eddie took the stage alone. That's why nobody wanted to follow Eddie—ever. That's also why, despite the last-minute scheduling adjustment, the announcement of his participation sparked a rush of people.

Eddie took the stage after a few excellent opening performances, and the audience went crazy. For two hours, America's most exciting entertainer captivated thousands of people. They cheered and wept, and when Eddie finished, they applauded for fifteen minutes, genuinely moved and grateful to know that one day they would be able to tell their grandkids, "I was there the day Eddie made history."

Of course they did. Their descendants continue to tell their children the same narrative. Because, remember, it was the 1960s. When America was at war, young people felt rebellious. A time when a farmer called David had the foresight to recognize that the fields surrounding his hometown would be ideal for his carefully prepared celebration of love and unity. Of course, he was correct. A few months before, another type of gathering took place in the same location, bringing 175,000 young people together for three days of terrible slaughter. An enormous carnage left 50,000 Americans dead or injured. Many of them remained scattered, in awful fragments, on David's front lawn.

That's why, after three months of horrific cleansing, David was decided to dedicate the acreage surrounding his house to those who were buried beneath it. And he did. But unless you were there to hear the bands play their dirges, the choirs sing their hymns, to smell the air, still rank with rotting flesh, and listen to Eddie deliver his 13,000-word eulogy from memory, it's difficult to imagine what happened in that small town up north during that unforgettable summer of death.

Funny how things work out. Edward Everett was once regarded as America's greatest orator. But today, few people remember him at all. Fewer even remember a single sentence from the great speech he made so skillfully on that sacred afternoon in 1863. No one remembers David Wills, the man who arranged the event that converted the farmland around his house into the enormous National Cemetery we know today. But everyone remembers the man who stole the show seven score and sixteen years ago. A haggard man suffering from sickness and mourning the death of his son. A humble man, as far from a diva as a politician could get. An honest man who was content to write his speech on the morning of the event in David Wills' spare bedroom at home.

A man named Lincoln supplied the address that we all remember: a well-known address derived from a small hamlet up north. A small town called Gettysburg.

I met a millennial one day on the terrible streets of San Francisco and asked him what these letters signified.

"Too long, didn't read."

"You're kidding," I replied. "Why would someone with no time take time to tell me that they had no time?"

The millennial shrugged and replied, "People are busy?"

"I understand that," I answered. "But if you have time to spell out the fact that you're too busy to read what I wrote, how busy can you really be?"

However, the millennial was no longer listening. He leaned down to pet Freddy, who hissed angrily and attempted to bite his finger off. That caught the millennial's interest.

"Hi, dude! You should tell everyone your dog is cruel!"

"I'm sorry," I replied. "I didn't have time."

I wonder whether Freddy is smarter than he lets on. He made his case quickly, much as Lincoln did at Gettysburg. With a growl and a snap, he left an impression on his audience. My dog appears to grasp the value of brevity. But, do I? Have I had your attention so far? Or have I been droning on like Edward Everett, overthinking things?

Don't get me wrong: what Everett accomplished at Gettysburg was incredible. He penned 13,000 words, remembered them, and delivered them beautifully to a packed audience. His performance was regarded as a success by both the Union and the Confederacy. This was a man who could have talked about a pencil for eight minutes, or eighty, and for that, I have the highest regard. But I wonder how Everett would fare in our TL/DR culture. I wonder how he'd fare at a TED conference.

You might be acquainted with TED, a series of gatherings in Silicon Valley where self-proclaimed "creatives" pay thousands of dollars to hear luminaries speak on themes close to their hearts.

I titled my lecture "The Changing Face of the Modern-Day Proletariat" and spent my eighteen minutes onstage reflecting about castration, notably the oral castration of infant lambs. The seminar was well-attended. You may view it on YouTube right now. Yes, you should. Go ahead; I will wait.

Are you back? Great. As you can see, eating the testicles off a baby lamb isn't as savage as you might expect. Sure, it's disgusting, but it's a lot more pleasant than the procedure advocated by Humane Society specialists, who informed me that tying a tight rubber band around the scrotum is the best option. That approach takes days and produces extended anguish for the lamb, but it appears far more civilized than the toothier method. It is "approved." But it is not more effective. It is not any better for the lamb.

Anyway, I told my experience in far greater depth than my audience could have expected. Naturally, I cast myself as the protagonist.

I liked the concept of utilizing Aristotle's lofty language to explain the unexpected truth of eating the balls off infant lambs. But let me tell you, I would have preferred two hours rather than eighteen minutes to explain myself.

You might be surprised to learn that many TED Talks last longer than expected. Take it from someone who has sat through three days of these things: otherwise smart people have a difficult time keeping their stories under eighteen minutes. These are the TED Talks that are never put on YouTube. The ones that made me feel better about the difficulties I faced with mine. In fact, despite my best efforts, I went over the permitted time by two minutes. Not a big thing, right? Except that Lincoln only needed two minutes to reconcile a divided country—to immortalize the moment with words that we now regard as timeless.

Words that, if put on Facebook today, would almost certainly prompt a "TL/DR" from those with only a few seconds to spare.

Perhaps a "Woof!" from Freddy.

Chapter 27: SOMETHING UNFORGETTABLE AND REAL

A high-performance convertible flies down a two-lane highway at speeds well in excess of the posted limits. In hot pursuit, a professional stuntman drives a Ford station wagon that's pulling an empty trailer. The scene couldn't be simpler: No special effects, no CGI, just a good, old-fashioned Hollywood car chase.

On his deathbed, thirty-one years later, Bill Hickman recalls the scene in vivid detail. In his mind's eye, he can still see the convertible rounding the corner and disappearing from view. He can still feel the frustration at not being able to catch up. If he had been driving his famous Dodge Charger that day—the muscle car he drove in Bullitt—things might have ended differently.

Bill smiles at the memory. The Charger had been one hell of a car and Bullitt one hell of a movie. As the film's stunt coordinator, Bill had been asked to create the most realistic car chase ever filmed. By most accounts he'd done just that. Their muscle cars literally flew through the air.

It was the mistakes, though—along with the actual stunts—that brought a new sense of realism to every Bill Hickman sequence. In one shot, Bill sideswipes a parked car with a camera affixed to it, knocking it sideways. Normally, footage like that would wind up on the cutting room floor, but Bill argued that the mistake made the chase feel more real, and the director agreed. The shot stayed in, and Bullitt won an Oscar.

Following that, every director in Hollywood desired a car chase with the "Hickman touch." In The Seven-Ups, Bill drove his Pontiac Grand Ville so recklessly that the actor in the passenger seat screamed in terror. That wasn't in the script. But the director kept it in because it was authentic.

During The French Connection, a parked car's door opens seconds before Bill drives by at 60 mph, wrenching the door off its hinges. This, too, appears disturbingly real—because it is.

In the same scene, Hickman—doubling Gene Hackman—chases down a bad guy who has commandeered an El train in Brooklyn. The action takes place fifty feet below the fast train, with Hickman's 1971 Pontiac LeMans attempting to keep up on a busy New York street. It was a challenging sequence to shoot, and the director disliked the first take. He informed Hickman that he wanted a vehicle chase that would terrify the crap out of audiences, something memorable and authentic.

Bill smiles ruefully as he recalls his identical exchange with the famed director.

"You want real?" he asked. "See you tomorrow morning at the corner of Eighty-sixth and Stillwell. Bring your camera, if you're brave enough. "I will show you something real." The next morning, William Friedkin strapped himself and his camera into the back seat of Hickman's LeMans and shot some of the most terrifying video ever seen on TV. Why? Hickman exceeded 90 mph in actual New York City traffic. No special effects. There is no CGI. And no permit. What was the result? The French Connection won six Oscars, and Friedkin, the director of The Exorcist, described the sequence as "the scariest thing I've ever seen."

Bill can still see the convertible coming around the turn and disappearing from view. He still feels frustrated at not being able to catch up. And he can still imagine the scene that will greet him when he finally turns that corner: slumped behind the wheel of the damaged sports car, he sees the young driver who should have been sitting beside him. A driver's Porsche should have been fastened on the empty trailer behind his station wagon as they headed to the Salinas Speedway. Unfortunately, the boy insisted on driving himself to warm up the engine for the race he was supposed to run that afternoon.

It was a scene, sure, but this wasn't a movie, and without a director to declare "cut," the action unfolded in slow motion, as it sometimes does in real life. Bill dashed to the wreck and rescued his young protégé from the flaming pile of twisted steel. There were no final words. No final close-ups. Just the sound of one final exhale, seconds before the driver died in Bill's arms and everything went black.

That was the start of a legendary career—the career of a stuntman known for his preoccupation with making action films feel unforgettable and real—as well as the beginning of a legend. The legend of a twenty-four-year-old race car driver whose brief appearance on the big screen is regarded as genuine and unforgettable. James Dean was a rebel without a cause.

How bizarre: just a few weeks before the disaster, James Dean made a public service announcement urging young drivers to slow down. He looked into the camera and stated, "The life you save just might be mine." Then, just two hours before the fatal incident, a cop pulled him over and issued him a speeding ticket. Do you believe the world was trying to tell him something?

I do not know. I doubt Bill Hickman knew. But I can tell you this: back in 2002, I wasn't looking for clues from the universe. Every night, I was too busy impersonating an Evening Magazine host.

"Good evening, everyone! I'm Mike Rowe, and tonight we're at the Mondavi Vineyard in lovely Napa Valley, home of the world's greatest wines!"

"Good evening, everyone! I'm Mike Rowe, and tonight we're visiting the Snodgrass Apple Orchard in beautiful Pescadero, home of the best apples in the world!"

"Good evening, everyone! I'm Mike Rowe, and tonight we're visiting Eddie's Electronic Emporium in gorgeous downtown Burlingame, where you can get a great deal on your new big-screen TV!"

Never mind Steve McQueen cruising the tough streets of San Francisco in his souped-up Mustang. Instead, imagine a 42-year-old B-list celebrity racing down the same streets in a Lincoln Navigator (Evening Magazine's Official SUV!) loaded with swag: free champagne, free apples, free TVs—free everything I could get my hands on.

"Good evening, everyone! I'm Mike Rowe, and tonight we're coming to you from Futon World in beautiful Alameda, home of the Bay Area's finest futons!"

Do you know how difficult it is to strap a free futon to the roof of your free Navigator?

The truth is, for a guy who had lost all of his money, starring in a show like Evening was just what the doctor prescribed. I received free tickets to every concert in town, free nights in expensive hotels, free meals at five-star restaurants, and free clothing from Macy's (the Official Provider of Mike Rowe's Wardrobe!). It was similar to QVC, but this time I got to keep everything I was selling, including my aforementioned huge head cast in bronze. Not the most rewarding experience, but I wasn't looking for purpose. I was simply trying to get back on my feet, and all this free stuff made me feel a lot better—until one day, the universe called. Fortunately, I picked up the phone.

"Oh. Hello, Mom. "How is it going?"

"Well, your father is up on the roof, doing God knows what, and I'm worried he'll fall off. But I am fine."

My mother has never answered this straightforward question without first explaining what my father was doing. Then she got to the point.

"I am phoning regarding your granddad. He's 90 years old and won't be around forever. I was thinking how lovely it would be if, just once, he could turn on his television and see you doing something that appeared to be work."

Mothers. They can be really cruel.

"Well, thank you, Mom. What did you have in mind?

"Oh, I don't know," she replied. "What about a logging camp?" Or a dairy farm? Or even a coal mine?

"This is California, Mom. "Coal is illegal out here."

"Well, I'm sure you'll come up with something," she told me. "Where are you shooting this evening?"

"I believe tonight's episode will be coming to you from a Tea Room in Chinatown."

"Oh my," she remarked. "That sounds exciting. "Your grandfather will be riveted."

That night, I drove home from Chinatown with my Navigator brimming with complimentary tins of Jasmine Dragon Pearls (Evening Magazine's Official Tea!). I reflected about our chat along the way. It had been a long since I'd spoken with my father, and I missed him. Surely, there was space in our show for a piece he could relate to. Why not shake things up a little?

So, the next morning, after a free haircut at Diepetro/Todd (The Official Hair Stylists of Evening Magazine!), I drove about San Francisco, hoping to observe the city through my grandfather's eyes. There were no lumber camps, dairy farms, or mines of any description. Just boutiques, cafés, and other craft offerings. But the solution to my mother's inquiry was right under my feet. I didn't realize it was there all along.

Now, as he lies dying, Bill realizes an unavoidable truth about his own identity: his entire life has been one big vehicle pursuit. He also reflects on how fortunate he has been over the years. It's a miracle that no one has ever been injured in any of his scenes—unless you consider the very first scene, thirty-one years ago, when Bill was a young stuntman driving a station wagon, carrying an empty trailer, and attempting to keep up with that fast convertible.

Chapter 28: THE STAR OF THE SHOW

Our hero was knee-deep in a putrid river, far below the metropolis where he lived. Branson, his devoted videographer, accompanied him, as did his guide—a sewer inspector whose name he didn't know. The men were wearing orange overalls, rubber hip boots, and yellow hardhats. The inspector carried a bucket suspended from a rope wrapped around his neck. Our hero followed, while Branson trailed behind, dragged down by his camera and a microphone hooked to a long pole.

"Be careful," the inspector said. "It's as smooth as snot through here. If you slide, it is preferable to fall backwards."

"How much further?" our hero exclaimed.

"Not far," the inspector replied. "Another hundred yards."

The group descended farther into the labyrinth. The tunnel shortened, and the lights on their helmets illuminated red brick walls that appeared to undulate in the darkness. Was our hero hallucinating? Was it a trick of the light, or a phantom caused by the odor? No. It was cockroaches. Millions of roaches feast on a constant layer of human waste. Like moths to a flame, they swarmed over to greet the men, engulfing our hero in a blanket of rippling vermin. He felt disgusted, yet determined to do his task. And then, turning to Branson's camera, he addressed his audience:

"Good evening, folks…"

But he didn't get very far before a thumb-sized bug climbed into his mouth, forcing him to gag and splutter.

"Try not to talk," the inspector said. "Nothing good happens down here when your mouth is open."

This, too, was wonderful counsel, but our hero could not follow it because talking was his profession, and the sound of his own voice captivated him. Turning back to Branson's camera, he started again:

"Funny thing about sewers," he began, but never got to the punchline. A blast of coffee-colored wastewater had erupted from a small hole in the wall, shellacking the bonnier side of his sculpted face.

"See what I mean?" the inspector asked.

Strange popping sounds filled the air when the toilets on Nob Hill above them were flushed. Liquids exploded left and right from hidden pipes known as "laterals." Our hero had a thorough understanding of laterals. Before entering the sewer, he had loaded his head with all types of effluvia to share with his audience. That, too, was part of his job: knowing everything there was to know about diverse subjects and sharing his knowledge.

But the sewer did not cooperate.

The men continued, duck-walking through this shooting gallery of human scat. Pushing through the muck. Pushing through the mire. Splashing their way through a three-dimensional fresco of macrobiotic destruction that only Dante could have imagined. Finally, they rounded a bend and came to a crossroads where two tunnels met.

"This whole area needs work," the inspector stated, wiping away an army of roaches from the ceiling. "Do you see these rotten bricks in the archway? They all need to come out."

But our hero wasn't listening. He was peering back into Branson's camera lens and clearing his throat.

"The walls around me were built in 1866," he stated in a clear, well-modulated baritone. "And today, you'll find over a thousand miles of tunnels down here, all of which—"

Just then, a sewer rat sprang from the miasma and sneaked up behind him, as rats frequently do. He was the size of a shoebox, plump, wet, and smelled like urine. In an instant, the rodent scampered across our hero's back and up to his shoulder. He paused, perched like a parrot, shrieked into our hero's ear, and sank onto his lap. Squealing, our hero jumped to his feet, bashed his head into the low ceiling, and then collapsed face-first into the sludge as a curtain of roaches rained down on him.

Never mind Dante. This was a page only Poe could have written. A portrait only Bosch could have painted. This was a baptism in the river of excrement.

Our hero heaved himself up from the mud, trying to remember the distinction between hepatitis A and B. Not that it mattered; he'd undoubtedly contracted both. For once, he remained mute. However, the sewer inspector was not.

"Hello, Chief. When you're done messing around with the local wildlife, I could use some assistance over here. Would you grab that trowel and mix me a new batch of grout?"

The hero sighed. Why not? The sewer had stopped him at each turn. If he couldn't perform his own job, could he do someone else's?

"Thanks," the inspector replied, accepting the trowel.

For the first time, our hero gave the inspector a serious look. The man was in his late thirties and had blond hair. He was sweating profusely and breathing rapidly, yet he remained cheerful. His name was Gene. It says so directly on his work shirt.

"Please tell me they pay you a fortune."

The inspector grinned as he pounded his chisel deep into the rotten grout.

"I wouldn't call it a fortune," he stated, "but I'm doing pretty well."

"How is the smell? "Do you ever get used to it?"

"A man can get used to anything," Gene explained.

For the following hour, our hero forgot about the camera and served as the inspector's apprentice. He hammered out the brickwork. The true star was Gene, the modest sewer inspector who worked with him.

Thus began a new chapter in the life of our humiliated hero, who was inspired at that moment to develop a new type of entertainment. A show with a mission instead of a script, and a guest rather than a presenter. Unless you opt to go back to the beginning, which would be extremely satisfying for our hero...

Anyway, that is how I heard it.

Do you see what I did there? I transformed myself into a hero. You should try it sometime. Simply place yourself on a pedestal and write about yourself in the third person. But be careful—when you present yourself as the hero of your own show, it's tempting to dismiss everyone else as minor characters in your own tale. That is what occurred to me.

That would have made my father proud.

Speaking of heroes, at the beginning of this book, I vowed to revisit Paul Harvey—and, as I may have remarked, a promise made is a debt repaid. So, let me get right to it: Paul Harvey was a hero of mine. He was the son of a cop who was killed by two criminals, and he worked his way up from being an office boy at a radio station in Tulsa, Oklahoma, to hosting the popular radio show that inspired my podcast. For thirty-three years, he told us The Rest of the Story, and from what I recall, he always prioritized his themes.

Obviously, I cannot fill Paul Harvey's shoes. But I can follow in his footsteps, and I've attempted to do so in these pages by writing about the people that fascinate me the most. Unfortunately, many of those folks have died, including several I knew personally. Joan Rivers, Dick Clark, and Anthony Bourdain can no longer tell their own story. They, like Fred King, are now only remembered by me and the many individuals they impacted. I am grateful to have known them all.

Kippy Stroud, too, has died. I did not know her well, but I was delighted to spend a year in her spooky mansion.

Happily, my dog, Freddy, is still alive and well as of this writing, and mostly continental. So are my beloved parents, John and Peggy. Dad is still volunteering at the hospital, delivering Meals on Wheels, and prancing around on stage. Mom is still checking for mistakes on my Facebook page while working on her second book. May they continue to do so for another century.

Sandy is still upset with the Russians for sending Laika into space, but she is thrilled to see me publish a real book. "Nice to see you finally write something you get paid for," she tells me. "Think anybody'll read it?"

That is a very good question.

Chuck Klausmeyer, my high school classmate, still wears the horrible blue jacket he loaned me twenty years ago, even though it no longer fits. He also produces my show, despite my repeated warnings against working for old pals. Similarly, the Irish Hammer is still on the case, doing her best to keep me from turning into an asshole—or, worse, appearing like one. This last chapter, for example, has resulted in some friendly probing.

"Tell me," she asks, "will you refer to yourself in the third person from now on?" Will you need a new pedestal? And what shall I call you? "Do you prefer 'My Hero' or 'Your Majesty'?"

I've assured her that either is acceptable.

Grumpy's remains, but Johnny's is vanished, and Baltimore has suffered as a result. Unfortunately, the Baltimore Opera Company has also closed. Michael Gellert, my friend who helped me get through my first audition, now runs the Harbor City Music Company, one of the world's top a cappella women's choruses. The Chesapeake Chorus still exists, presently conducted by Fred King's son, Kevin. The old guard is mostly gone, but a new generation of guys is singing the same songs in four-part harmony at a loudness comparable to that of a Metallica performance.

Evening Magazine ceased broadcasting shortly after I left CBS to work on Dirty Jobs. I'm told that my departure and the show's downfall were entirely coincidental. QVC, on the other hand, is still going strong, reaching over 100 million homes and producing billions of dollars in revenue each year. I haven't always talked highly of my time there, but the truth is that I learnt everything I needed to know about the company there. For that, I am grateful. Perhaps I should also thank the rat. We're no longer in touch, but thanks to his prompt intervention, I ended up with more than just a successful show. I ended up with a solid foundation and what appears to be a promising career.

Speaking of rats, the trusted financial adviser who stole my money was ultimately sentenced to prison, and appropriately so. But I can't say I was an entirely innocent victim. Deep down, I thought the figures he presented were too wonderful to be true, but I buried my head in the sand and told myself the story I wanted to hear. I've learned my lesson.

I also committed to tell you the truth, as I heard it. And for the most part, I believe I have. But, of course, the truth and the complete truth are never the same—which gets us back to Phil Harris. He had a huge stroke in 2010, and died in a hospital bed, unable to speak. Todd Stanley, the videographer who had been following him for years, was there with him. Todd turned his camera off out of respect. But Phil motioned Todd to his bedside and wrote a few words on a scrap of paper: "You've got to get the end of the story."

So Todd Stanley grabbed up his camera, and the millions of people who had been able to see Phil's life joined together to mourn his passing. Isn't that extraordinary? Even... heroic?

Phil Harris believed that a story was incomplete unless it had a conclusion.

Paul Harvey thought that a tale was not complete until you heard the rest of it.

I believe both were correct.

Regarding Paul Harvey and the rest of his story: He died a year before Phil Harris. He was one of the few broadcasters who ever received the Presidential Medal of Freedom. I recently heard from his kid. Paul Harvey Jr. wrote and produced The Rest of the Story for his father, and when his letter arrived in my office, I was frightened to open it. For all I knew, it was a cease and desist order for my podcast.

But it wasn't. It was a very sweet note, accompanied by a large cheque for the mikeroweWORKS Foundation. According to Paul Jr., his father would have appreciated the work we were doing. Putting modesty aside, it was a proud and humbling moment for me— another reason to be grateful.

Finally, a clarification regarding Jon Stewart. I mentioned his name before because I intended to come back later and tell you about the two times I was hired to anchor The Daily Show. It's an intriguing story, but my friend Alex (a wreck of a man and an excellent writer) claims that my book is already too long. His instincts have been useful—so far, at least—so I'll save that for another day. Instead, I'll just mention, for the record, that I met Jon Stewart once, way back in 2006. I appeared on The Daily Show, answering Jon's trenchant and intelligent questions. "So tell us, Mike, what was your dirtiest job?"

According to what I heard, Jon Stewart described my response as "the funniest thing he'd ever heard." However, you may watch our interview on YouTube and decide for yourself.

In fact, I believe you should.

Go ahead. Google it.

I will wait...

Chapter 29: CHARLIE'S BIG BREAK

Charlie realized he had a hit the moment he took up the guitar. The melody appeared to write itself. The words came out of his mouth as if he'd known them his entire life. Charlie, like every other young musician who had arrived to Los Angeles with big dreams, needed a break—a opportunity to show everyone who he was and what he could do.

Finally, that chance has arrived.

Seated across from him were two key personalities in the music industry: the Legendary Drummer, who had befriended him a few weeks before, and the Legendary Producer, who is credited with establishing the "California Sound." Either man could have made Charlie famous overnight.

Charlie touched the neck of his acoustic guitar, took a deep breath, and started playing. And things couldn't have gone better. The legendary producer nodded along with the music. The Legendary Drummer murmured in harmony. The legendary drummer replied, "Hell, yeah!" The Legendary Producer exclaimed, "Damn." "Let us make an album."

So they did.

Charlie spent the next several weeks recording four original tunes. Charlie discovered the magic that every successful artist strives for in the studio with the assistance of the Legendary Drummer and two of his Legendary Bandmates. However, the Legendary Producer took problem with some of the lyrics. He preferred something "softer." Something more "relatable."

Charlie, like any great artist, was unwilling to compromise his work. He pushed back.

In simply, Charlie blew it. He alienated those he needed the most. The Legendary Producer stopped answering calls. The Legendary Drummer returned to become a rock star.

Charlie took it hard and, by all accounts, handled the rejection quite poorly. After being ignored for weeks, he addressed the Legendary Drummer at his Sunset Boulevard house. He had brought a gift: a single bullet.

"What's this for?" inquired the Legendary Drummer.

"It's for you," Charlie stated. "Every time you look at it, I want you to think how nice it is that your kids are still safe."

That did it. The Legendary Drummer did not take threats lightly, especially ones directed at his family. Charlie should have known that. So the Legendary Drummer battered Charlie, just like the drums he played for a living. Then he threw Charlie to the floor and beat him even harder. He pounded Charlie until he cried like a baby. But the hardest blow was yet to come.

One year later, Charlie, who was broke and unemployed, was passing time in a record shop. He noticed a poster of the Legendary Drummer performing onstage with his Legendary Brothers. They released a new track called "Bluebirds over the Mountains," a rendition of an old rockabilly tune.

"Jesus," Charlie exclaimed, "what a bunch of hacks." They don't even write their own music anymore.

The B-side, titled "Never Learn Not to Love," was an original. Charlie was naturally curious. They'd modified the title. They had changed some of the lyrics. But the rest was identical! It was the same song he had auditioned with, but now it was sung by the Legendary Drummer, Dennis Wilson.

No one knows if having his music stolen by the Beach Boys pushed Charlie over the brink. But no one can deny that in the months that followed, Charlie paid a visit to the house of that Legendary Producer, Terry Melcher. Melcher subsequently relocated to Malibu, which was fantastic for him but not so good for the new residents of his former home. Those people were all slain in the most heinous manner possible.

For whatever it's worth, Charlie's audition song was initially titled "Cease to Exist," which he refused to change. Long after his Legendary Drummer and Legendary Producer had passed away, Charlie lay rotting in his jail cell, waiting for the big break that never seemed to arrive—until it did, forty-six years later. Charles Manson, a mass murderer, was ultimately brought to justice after a significant breakthrough.

"Never Learn Not to Love." See what the Beach Boys did there? With the careful use of a single double negative, Manson's "Cease to Exist" sounds considerably less crazy and far more like a Zen koan. During my audition for No Relation, Dick Clark advised me to avoid greeting everyone.

I was confused: what did that mean? My expression reflected my perplexity.

"When you looked into the lens," he explained, "your first words were 'Hello, everyone.'" That is perhaps not the finest way to say hello."

"It's not?"

"No. And saying, 'It's good to see you all again,' is also a mistake."

"It is?"

"Yes. People do not perceive themselves as part of a mob, Mike. They perceive themselves as individuals. They seek a personal relationship with someone they can trust. Your job is to be that person. This is what a good host does. He becomes a guest at the viewer's house."

"When you speak to the camera, Mike, don't think of everyone. Think about one person. Somebody you know. Someone you like. Talk with them. And if you say, 'It's good to see you again,' make damn sure you mean it."

"Thank you, Mr. Clark." "I will do that."

"You can call me Dick," he explained. "All my friends do."

The next day, Tom Frank called me again; it had come down to me and one other guy—the young lad with the pearly teeth and strange tan.

Perhaps it was Chuck's fortunate blue jacket. Perhaps they flipped a coin. I'm not sure, but I was chosen to host No Relation. We shot forty episodes that summer on the same set as The Price Is Right. I shared a dressing room with Bob Barker. (Not at the same time, obviously.) We may have shot another season, but No Relation was canceled, as I had feared. Tom Frank was beside himself. He still refers to the show as Hola, Acapulco!, the destination for all of our contestants.

I sometimes wonder if No Relation would have been a success if Dick Clark had hosted and produced it. I bet he could have pointed those dimwitted celebs in the proper direction. He was, after all, an excellent broadcaster. A host who was essentially a guest. A ghostly visitor. A ghost on my screen who always appeared delighted to see me—even though I knew he couldn't.

Tom Frank may not be the most well-known person in town, but he has done well.

Chapter 30: BOBBY BRINGS HOME THE BACON

Britney Spears forgot to thank the pig during the Grammy Awards. No one called her out on it, but in retrospect, the facts are clear: without that pig, Britney would never have sold 100 million CDs. No way. Similarly, Steven Spielberg would never have brought Jurassic Park to the big screen, and Neil Armstrong would never have walked on the moon. However, none of these individuals ever acknowledged the pig. Bobby, on the other hand? He thought about the pig every day. Why shouldn't he? Bobby died with a $3.2 billion net worth and a product that revolutionized the industry.

Bobby was mostly a tinkerer and risk taker. But not always in that sequence. When he was twelve, he made a box kite, tied it to his back, and plunged off the top of Grinnell College in Iowa, just to test if he could fly. It turned out he could. For approximately thirty seconds.

There was also the time he bolted a propeller to the back of his sled and powered it with an engine from an old washing machine. It turned out that motorized sleds do not fly, either. However, they travel quicker than traditional sleds. Much faster.

Bobby was a tinkerer, you know. A risk-taker. But not always in that sequence. And not only as a boy. When he was twenty-one, he offered to find the guest of honor for a fraternity luau. There were numerous options to pick from. The farmer wouldn't miss even one swine, would he?

Not twelve hours later, the guest of honor was slowly turning over an open fire, roasted to a crispy golden brown and holding an apple in its teeth. According to all accounts, the luau was a huge success—but Bobby awoke the next day with a moral hangover. What had he been thinking? The pig was not his to take, but he took it. As the son of a pastor, he ought to have known better. So Bobby returned to the burgled pigpen, admitted his wrongdoing to the farmer, and promised to reimburse him.

Who knows what our world would be like today if the farmer had let go of the past? But, of course, the farmer didn't, because stealing a pig in Iowa in 1948 was equivalent to rustling cattle in Colorado a century before. It was larceny, especially at Grinnell, where any physics student could tell you that every action had an equal and opposite reaction. The farmer, as a good Christian, pardoned Bobby's transgression. But he still needed to file charges. Despite like Bobby, the sheriff had to arrest him. Even though the college's dean admired Bobby, he had to expel him.

Grant Gale, a physics professor at Grinnell College, came to Bobby's rescue. He begged the dean, the sheriff, the mayor, and all the good people in town to reconsider the sentence for pork theft and find a punishment appropriate to the crime.

In the end, the farmer dropped the accusations, the sheriff relented, and Bobby's expulsion was reduced to a one-semester suspension.

For some pupils, that could have meant a four-month holiday, but not for Bobby.

The professor was intrigued. He utilized one of the prototypes to demonstrate electron flow through a solid in what turned out to be the first academic solid-state electronics course ever offered. What about the other prototype? That ended up in the hands of the suspended senior, who enjoyed tinkering and taking chances. But not always in that sequence.

You see, if Bobby hadn't spent innumerable hours working with that prototype—the first transistor created by Bell Labs—there would have been no little step for Neil Armstrong, because Apollo 11 would have lacked an onboard computer. Without computer-generated imagery, Steven Spielberg's Jurassic Park would not have been. Britney Spears would not have received any Grammy Awards if there had been no Auto-Tune.

The entire intricacies of Bobby's transformation of the modern era would fill a book, one best described by a physicist or someone who truly understands how the universe works. But I can explain this: without Bobby's willingness to take risks, all of his tinkering would have been for naught—because if you think diving off a roof attached to a homemade kite is risky, try starting a start-up in Silicon Valley before the silicon even exists.

That is the legacy of Robert Noyce, a man who enjoyed tinkering and taking risks, but not necessarily in that order. But don't forget Bob's silent partner: a 25-pound suckling pig whose influence on our lives began with a fleeting appearance at a long-forgotten luau in America's heartland. The microchip, a tiny bit of silicon, was created by the sacrifice of a pig.

Forty years after Robert Noyce threw a pig on a spit and changed the world—one year before I put a pig on a pedestal and changed my blue jeans—another Robert was doing things with pigs that couldn't be overlooked. So, they weren't. This Robert became the most popular character we ever had on Dirty Jobs. What about his pigs? They accomplished what armies of tourists and gamblers could not.

For fifty years, Bob Combs drove his vintage pickup truck up and down the Las Vegas strip, loading it with uneaten buffet food from high-end hotels and casinos before returning to his small farm in north Las Vegas. In an otherwise ordinary backyard, he shoveled the treasures into a gigantic cooker, a towering, Rube Goldberg-esque contraption that transported the buffet into a giant stewpot three floors above ground. It was hardly high-tech, but it worked. The grub was quickly reduced to a thick, brownish bouillabaisse.

Bob informed my field producer, Barsky, that the smell reminded him of a bakery.

He had built the entire gadget himself, using pieces salvaged from nearby junkyards. As a result, tons of uneaten people food—waste that would otherwise end up in a landfill—ended up filling his farm's troughs. Thanks to Bob, a city with excessive traffic now has a conservation program to brag about.

I accompanied Bob as he drove that antique pickup down from the cooker to the troughs, boiling slop splattering over the roof, down the windshield, and onto the hood. Barsky's eyes widened as hundreds of hungry pigs swooped on the leftovers. I can still hear the shrieking and slurping that accompanied this raucous and gluttonous spectacle. It was epic. Simply... awesome.

Even now, people ask me about Bob Combs. I tell them he was a cross between Jimmy Stewart and Old MacDonald—the living embodiment of everything Dirty Jobs sought to highlight: a modest, good-humored man with a remarkable work ethic; a man who had discovered a new angle and prospered in a business with razor-thin margins. As grain prices soared, putting a strain on all of the farmers surrounding him, Bob continued to draw from his seemingly limitless store of leftovers. It was hard labor, to be sure, but it was beneficial to his business, the environment, and the city of Las Vegas. When we first met in 2006, Bob faced opposition from the HSUS, EPA, and OSHA, as well as neighbors who wanted to shut down his pig farm due to odor concerns.

Las Vegas was expanding, and hundreds of homeowners did not want a pig farm so close to their brand-new houses. They didn't care that Bob had been around for decades. They didn't care that Bob was performing an important public service. They just worried about the smell—and getting rid of it.

Developers reacted angrily. Committees are constituted. Petitions were circulated, and hearings were conducted. The pressure to close Bob's farm was relentless, but Bob stood firm, and I'm glad he did, because when the Dirty Jobs show aired, the developers took a different approach: they pooled their resources and offered to buy Bob's property. They offered him a stunning sum of 75 million dollars.

Bob died.

"Bob," I answered. "What are your thoughts?" It costs 75 million dollars."

Bob said, "Yes. But what will I do with my pigs?

"I don't know," I replied. "Kill them?" Eat them? "You're going anyway, right?"

Bob had nothing to say about that. But later, I realized that his genuine query wasn't, "What would I do with my pigs?" It was, "What would I do without them?"

Bob Combs had put his pigs on a pedestal long before I came along. He recognized what was most important to him. It was the labor, you see. Work that would have halted if he had taken the money. Even though he was reaching the age of eighty, his work defined him. He was simply unwilling to forsake his work.

"I kinda like the smell," he explained. "I guess I've gotten used to it."

The contents of this book may not be copied, reproduced or transmitted without the express written permission of the author or publisher. Under no circumstances will the publisher or author be responsible or liable for any damages, compensation or monetary loss arising from the information contained in this book, whether directly or indirectly. .

Disclaimer Notice:

Although the author and publisher have made every effort to ensure the accuracy and completeness of the content, they do not, however, make any representations or warranties as to the accuracy, completeness, or reliability of the content. , suitability or availability of the information, products, services or related graphics contained in the book for any purpose. Readers are solely responsible for their use of the information contained in this book

Every effort has been made to make this book possible. If any omission or error has occurred unintentionally, the author and publisher will be happy to acknowledge it in upcoming versions.

Made in United States
Troutdale, OR
12/29/2024

27415657R00080